Mastering Adjusting Entries

by Gary F. Bulmash, CPA, MBA, DBA

Associate Professor of Accounting
American University
Washington, D.C.

Gary F. Bulmash, CPA, MBA, DBA, is Associate Professor of Accounting and former Chairman, Department of Accounting, American University. Professor Bulmash has taught courses for AICPA. In addition to teaching, he has worked extensively with small businesses. He is author of *Tax Aspects of Being Self-Employed* (Prentice-Hall, 1981, revised 1988) and is recognized for outstanding achievement in *Who's Who in the East, 1982–83.*

© American Institute of Professional Bookkeepers, 2007
ISBN 978-1-884826-25-2

1207

INTRODUCTION

Mastering Adjusting Entries covers everything you need to know for the accruals and deferrals portion of the *Certified Bookkeeper* examination. If you take the optional open-book Final Examination at the end of this workbook, return the answer sheet to AIPB and achieve a grade of at least 70, then become a *Certified Bookkeeper* within 3 years, you will receive retroactively six (6) Continuing Professional Education Credits (CPECs) toward the *Certified Bookkeeper* continuing education requirements. You will also receive promptly an AIPB *Certificate of Completion*.

If you are not an applicant for the *Certified Bookkeeper* designation and take the optional open-book Final Examination at the end of this workbook, return the answer sheet to AIPB and achieve a grade of at least 70, you will receive an AIPB *Certificate of Completion*.

When you have completed this course, you should be able to:

1. Understand accruals and deferrals.

2. Calculate and record adjusting entries for accrued revenue and expenses.

3. Calculate and record adjusting entries for deferred revenue and expenses.

4. Construct an unadjusted trial balance, add the adjustments and complete the adjusted trial balance.

To get the most out of the course, we suggest the following:

1. Read the concise narrative that begins each section.

2. Read the narrative again. This time, cover the solution to each illustrative problem and try to figure it out yourself. *Actually write it out.* By trying to solve the problem and checking your answer against the correct solution, you will learn a great deal.

3. Take Quiz #1 at the end of each section to see what you learned and what you need to review.

4. Take Quiz #2 at the end of each section to master any points you may have missed.

Lastly, after completing the course, please take a moment to fill out the brief Course Evaluation at the back of your workbook (whether or not you take the final). It will help us to improve this and other courses.

Important: This course is current as of the date of publication, February 1, 2007. Because tax laws are always changing, double-check the changes in the tax law, new IRS pronouncements, and recent court cases that may affect the return.

Enjoy the course—and congratulations on taking a major step toward advancing your professional knowledge and career.

CONTENTS

Certified Bookkeeper Applicants

The best way to study for the certification exam is to take each section's quizzes over and over until you can answer questions quickly and comfortably—*and* know why the answer is correct. If you have trouble with a question, or know the answer, but not why it is correct, review the related material. Write answers on a separate sheet, wherever possible, to avoid seeing them each time you take the quiz.

Section 1

WHY WE USE ACCRUALS, DEFERRALS AND OTHER ADJUSTMENTS

Cash Basis Accounting

A small number of companies do their accounting on a cash basis. Generally, payments received (checks, cash, credit card, etc.) are income, and payments made are expenses. Cash basis businesses can almost produce an income statement from their checkbook, presenting total payments from customers as revenue and total disbursements as expenses. The kinds of businesses that use cash basis accounting include some professional practices (such as doctors, lawyers, accountants, and engineers) and other service businesses. If total revenues are higher than total expenses, the business has net income. If total expenses are higher than total revenues, the business has a net loss.

Accrual Basis Accounting

Most companies do their accounting on the accrual basis. This is the method required by generally accepted accounting principles (GAAP). GAAP prohibits recording an incoming payment as revenue unless you have *earned* it. But if you have earned the revenue, you *must* recognize it (record the revenue on your books) even if you have not received a single dollar of payment. If your customer sent you more revenue than you have earned— for example, the customer sent you a $10,000 advance, but you have earned only $4,000 of the payment—you can record as revenue only the portion that you earned, even though the rest is already in your bank.

Examples of Recording Revenue

EXAMPLE 1: Your consulting firm completes a $10,000 consulting assignment on December 1 and sends out the invoice to the customer, but the customer does not send you payment until January.

Under cash basis accounting, you cannot record any portion of the $10,000 as income this year because you did not receive any cash payment. Your income statement will not show any of the $10,000 as revenue.

Under accrual basis accounting, you *must* (you do not have a choice) recognize the $10,000 of revenue (record $10,000 of revenue on your books) for the year because you performed the service this year. Revenue earned, but not yet received, is accrued revenue. Your income statement will show that $10,000 as revenue even though you have not yet received it.

EXAMPLE 2: Your consulting firm receives a $10,000 advance in December, 20X0, but does not begin work until January, 20X1.

Under cash basis accounting, you recognize $10,000 revenue in 20X0 because that is what you received in cash. The $10,000 in revenue will appear on your income statement.

Under accrual basis accounting, you cannot recognize any of the $10,000 in 20X0 because you have not *earned* it. You must *defer* recognizing any of the $10,000 until your have *earned* it. None of the $10,000 will appear on your 20X0 income statement.

Examples of Recording Expenses

EXAMPLE 3: On December 1, 20X0, your consulting firm moves into new quarters for which it will pay $1,000 a month rent, with the first payment to be made in January, 20X1.

Under cash basis accounting, your company has $0 rent expense for 20X0 because it did not pay any cash for rent.

Under accrual basis accounting, your company recognizes (records) $1,000 rent expense because this is the amount of expense *incurred* (used up) for the month of December, 20X0. This $1,000 of rent expense will be included as an expense on your company's 20X0 income statement even though no payment was made for December's rent.

EXAMPLE 4: On December 1, your consulting firm pays $3,000 for 3 months' rent in advance, for December, January and February.

Under cash basis accounting, you have $3,000 of rent expense for this year because that is how much you paid out. Your income statement will show $3,000 as "rent expense."

Under accrual basis accounting, only $1,000 of your payment may be recorded in the Rent Expense account for December because you incurred (used up) only $1,000 this year. The $2,000 not yet used must be recorded to an asset account (such as Prepaid Rent or Rent Paid In Advance) until it is used up next year. That is, you must *defer* recognition of $2,000 as expense until later periods. Your income statement will show only the $1,000 used as "rent expense."

Of course, accruals and deferrals also affect the balance sheet. How accruals and deferrals are computed and recorded and how they affect the financial statements will be explained in this course.

QUIZ 1 **WHY WE USE ACCRUALS, DEFERRALS AND OTHER ADJUSTMENTS**

Problem I.

Multiple choice. Circle the correct answer.

1. Under accrual basis accounting, you recognize revenue . . .

    a. when you receive payment
    b. when you have earned the revenue
    c. when you have earned the revenue and received the payment
    d. when you have earned the revenue and received at least some of the payment

2. Under accrual basis accounting, you recognize an expense when you have . . .

    a. paid the expense
    b. incurred the expense and paid for it
    c. recorded payment of the expense on your books
    d. incurred the expense

3. Under accrual basis accounting, revenues presented on the income statement are . . .

    a. revenues earned during the year
    b. revenues earned for the year in cash
    c. cash received from customers during the year
    d. revenues earned during the year for which invoices have been sent to customers

4. Under accrual basis accounting, expenses presented on the income statement are . . .

    a. expenses incurred during the year
    b. expenses paid during the year
    c. expenses incurred during the year that have been paid
    d. payments to vendors for expenses incurred through December 31

QUIZ 1   Solutions and Explanations

1. b

Only in *cash* basis accounting do you recognize revenue when you receive payment.

2. d

In cash basis accounting, you recognize an expense only when you pay the expense.

3. a

The income statement simply presents the revenues recorded in the general ledger. Under accrual basis accounting, revenues in the general ledger are those earned, regardless of whether cash has been received.

4. a

The income statement simply presents the expenses recorded in the general ledger. Under accrual basis accounting, expenses in the general ledger are those incurred, regardless of whether cash has been paid.

QUIZ 2 WHY WE USE ACCRUALS, DEFERRALS AND OTHER ADJUSTMENTS

Problem I.

Multiple choice. Circle the correct answer.

1. To *accrue* revenue at year end is to record . . .

    a. receipt of payment from a customer
    b. the amount of an invoice sent to a customer
    c. an amount earned for which payment has not been received
    d. an amount earned and deposited in your bank

2. To *defer* revenue is to . . .

    a. postpone recording a customer's payment as revenue until it is earned
    b. postpone depositing a cash payment in the bank
    c. postpone accepting payment from a customer until you do the work
    d. postpone depositing a customer's payment to minimize current-year income taxes

3. To *accrue* an expense is to record . . .

    a. payment of the expense
    b. the portion of the expense used and paid for
    c. an expense incurred but not yet paid for
    d. the amount of a check sent to pay an expense

4. To *recognize* revenue or an expense is to . . .

    a. record the amount in the general ledger Revenue or Expense account
    b. deposit the revenue in the bank or pay the expense
    c. know that a particular cash payment received was revenue or that a cash payment made was an expense
    d. add the amount to company profits or losses

QUIZ 2   Solutions and Explanations

1. c

2. a

When you receive an advance payment and do not earn the full amount before year end, the unearned portion is kept in a separate account (that is, not in the Revenue account) until it is earned in the future.

3. c

Under GAAP, when you incur an expense (use it up) before you have paid it, the expense is still recognized and recorded in the appropriate Expense account.

4. a

ACCRUED REVENUE

Introduction

Accrued revenue is uncollected revenue, that is, revenue earned but not yet received. To put it another way, receipt of cash takes place after the revenue is earned and recorded on the books. Every adjusting entry for accrued revenue debits a receivable account, increasing assets on the balance sheet, and credits a revenue account, increasing revenue and net income on that period's income statement.

How to Record Accrued Revenue

The general entry to record accrued revenue is:

Accounts [or Other] Receivable	(balance sheet asset account)
Revenue	(income statement revenue account)
To accrue revenue earned	

Examples of Accrued Revenue

Examples of receivables include:

- Commissions and royalties earned, but not yet received.

    Commission [or Royalty] Receivable
    Commission [or Royalty] Revenue

- Interest earned on customers' notes and company investments in long-term bonds and short-term notes, but not yet received.

    Interest Receivable
    Interest Revenue

- Space leased to a tenant for a period for which rent has not yet been received.

    Rent Receivable
    Rent Revenue

How Failure to Accrue Revenue Affects the Financial Statements

Failure to record accrued revenue will have the following impacts on the financial statements:

- Assets will be understated on the balance sheet (because the omitted entry increases a receivable account);

- Revenues will be understated on the income statement (because the omitted entry increases a revenue account); and, as a result,

- Net income will be understated on the income statement.

Sample Problems

PROBLEM 1: A company with a year end of December 31 rents space to a tenant for $1,000 per month. The December rent has not been received as of December 31. What is the adjusting journal entry on December 31?

SOLUTION 1: Because 1 month's rent revenue of $1,000 has accrued, the adjusting journal entry on December 31 is:

Rent Receivable	1,000	
Rent Revenue		1,000

To accrue one month's rent revenue

Even though December's rent of $1,000 has not been received, the company has still earned it because the tenant used the space during December.

PROBLEM 2: LyCo contracts to sell widgets for a customer in return for a 10% commission on sales. As of LyCo's year end, the project has produced $140,000 in sales, but LyCo has received only $5,000 in commissions. What adjusting journal entry does LyCo record at year end?

SOLUTION 2: First, compute commissions due on the $140,000 in sales:

$140,000 x 10% = $14,000 commissions

Then compute commissions accrued (earned but not received) by deducting the payment received from the total earned:

$14,000 commissions earned – $5,000 received = $9,000 commissions accrued

To record the adjusting journal entry at year end:

Commission Receivable	9,000	
Commission Revenue		9,000
To accrue commission earned		

Accruing Interest Receivable

On a short-term note, interest accrues (builds up) and is usually received with payment of principal (face amount of the note) on the due date. On a long-term note, interest is received periodically rather than when the note is due. If the accounting period ends before the interest is received in cash, interest is accrued to the last day of that period.

The formula to compute the interest for a period is:

Face amount (principal) x annual interest rate x fraction of year = accrued interest

If your company converts a customer's overdue accounts receivable to a note, the customer will not pay either interest or principal until the note is due. When the accounts receivable is converted to a note, two entries are required. The first entry is to record the new note:

Note Receivable
    Accounts Receivable
To record conversion of A/R to N/R

The second entry is to accrue the first year's interest:

Interest Receivable
    Interest Revenue
To accrue monthly interest revenue

PROBLEM 3: XYZ Company holds a customer's $1,000, 90-day note, which is dated November 1 and bears interest of 12%. The company's year end is December 31. How much interest revenue is accrued as of December 31?

SOLUTION 3: Interest is stated on an annual basis unless otherwise specified on the loan document. As of December 31, interest has accrued for 2 months, November and December. Applying the formula to compute interest:

$1,000 face amount (principal) x 12% = $120 for the year/12 months = $10 per month interest x 2 months (November and December) = $20 accrued interest as of December 31

To record the accrued interest, the following adjusting entry is made in the general journal:

Interest Receivable	20	
Interest Revenue		20

To accrue 2 months' interest on $1,000, 12% note

PROBLEM 4: Mainstream Co., which has a year end of December 31, holds a customer's $2,000, 10% (interest per year), 1-year note due April 1, 20X2. The customer will repay the principal and all interest on the note's maturity (due) date. How much interest accrues as of December 31, 20X1, and what is the entry to record it?

SOLUTION 4: To compute interest accrued on December 31, 20X1: $2,000 principal x 10% interest = $200 annual interest x 9/12 months (for the 9 months April–December) = $150 interest accrued as of December 31. Mainstream records the following entry:

Interest Receivable	150	
Interest Revenue		150

To accrue 9 months' interest earned on $2,000, 10% note

QUIZ 1   ACCRUED REVENUE

Problem I.

Make the following adjusting journal entries:

1. Accrue interest revenue of $400

2. Accrue commission revenue earned of $1,400

3. Accrue rental revenue of $2,400

Problem II.

1. Your company holds a $50,000, 8% note receivable, interest payable annually on each June 30. When your company's fiscal year ends on August 31, 20X5, you have received no interest payment since June 30, 20X5. What adjusting journal entry do you make?

2. If your company's fiscal year ended on December 31, 20X5 and you had not received the interest payment since June 30, 20X5, what entry would you make?

Problem III.

Your company rents a machine to another company at an annual rental of $15,000. At year end, you have received $13,500 in rent. Record the adjusting journal entry.

Problem IV.

Fill in the blanks.

1. Accrued revenue is revenue _____ but not _____.

2. The adjusting entry to accrue revenue debits a(n) _____ account and credits a(n) _____ account.

3. If you omit the adjusting journal entry to accrue revenue, you _____ (overstate, understate) your firm's net income.

Problem V.

Multiple choice. Circle the correct answer.

1. Interest Receivable is what type of account?

    a. Asset
    b. Liability
    c. Revenue
    d. Expense

2. A company omitted its adjusting entry to accrue rental revenue. What effect does this have on liabilities at year end?

    a. overstate
    b. understate
    c. no effect
    d. it is not possible to know without more information

3. When revenue is accrued . . .

    a. cash is received when the revenue is recognized
    b. cash is received before the revenue is recognized
    c. cash is received after the revenue is recognized
    d. cash may be received before or after the revenue is recognized

QUIZ 1   *Solutions and Explanations*

Problem I.

    1. Interest Receivable   400

            Interest Revenue   400

            To accrue interest revenue

    2. Commission Receivable   1,400

            Commission Revenue   1,400

            To accrue commission earned

    3. Rent Receivable   2,400

            Rent Revenue   2,400

            To accrue rent revenue

Problem II.

    1. Interest Receivable   667

            Interest Revenue   667

            To accrue 2 months' interest on note ($50,000 x 8% x 2/12)

    2. Interest Receivable   2,000

            Interest Revenue   2,000

            To accrue 6 months' interest on note ($50,000 x 8% x 6/12)

Problem III.

    Rent Receivable   1,500

        Rent Revenue   1,500

        To accrue rental revenue

You have collected $13,500 of the $15,000 earned. Thus, the amount to accrue is $1,500 ($15,000 – $13,500).

Problem IV.

1. earned, received (collected)

2. asset (receivable), revenue

3. understate

Problem V.

1. a

Receivable means that cash will be received in the future, making this an asset account.

2. c

A liability is money that the company owes, not money that it collects. Thus, an adjusting entry related to revenue does not affect liabilities.

3. c

QUIZ 2   ACCRUED REVENUE

Problem I.

Make the following adjusting journal entries:

1. Accrued rent revenue of $3,600

2. Accrued interest revenue of $4,200

3. Accrued commission revenue of $2,800

4. Receipt in December of $2,000 in commissions earned and accrued in November

Problem II.

Your company holds DuCo's $60,000, 12% mortgage on which it has collected $7,000 in interest for the year. What adjusting entry do you record at year end?

Problem III.

Your company has a 60-day, $3,000, 12% note receivable dated December 1. What adjusting journal entry do you record on December 31 if you have received no interest payments?

Problem IV.

Multiple choice. Circle the correct answer.

1. Interest receivable appears on which financial statement?

   a. income statement
   b. balance sheet
   c. statement of capital
   d. statement of retained earnings

2. Accrued revenue is revenue . . .

    a. neither earned nor received
    b. received but not earned
    c. earned but not received
    d. earned and received

3. The adjusting entry to accrue revenue . . .

    a. increases the balance in the ledger Cash account
    b. decreases the balance in the ledger Cash account
    c. may increase or decrease the balance in the ledger Cash account
    d. does not affect the ledger Cash account

4. If you fail to record the adjusting entry to accrue revenue, it will affect the income statement as follows:

    a. net income will be understated
    b. revenue will be understated
    c. neither a nor b
    d. both a and b

QUIZ 2 Solutions and Explanations

Problem I.

1.	Rent Receivable	3,600	
	Rent Revenue		3,600
	To accrue rent revenue		

2.	Interest Receivable	4,200	
	Interest Revenue		4,200
	To accrue interest revenue		

3.	Commission Receivable	2,800	
	Commission Revenue		2,800
	To accrue commission revenue		

4.	Cash	2,000	
	Commission Receivable		2,000
	To record receipt of November commission		

Problem II.

Interest Receivable	200	
Interest Revenue		200
To accrue interest revenue		

You are entitled to $7,200 in interest for the year. To compute: $60,000 face amount x 12% = $7,200 interest for the year – $7,000 received = $200 accrued interest (that is, interest that you will receive)

Problem III.

Interest Receivable	30	
Interest Revenue		30

To accrue 1 month's interest earned on note ($3,000 x 12% x 1/12)

The adjusting entry accrues 1 month's interest. Although the note is for 60 days, the interest rate is stated as an annual rate and therefore must be divided by 12 to find the interest that has accrued for 1 month.

Problem IV.

1. b

Because interest receivable is an asset.

2. c

It is recognized (booked) as revenue because it has been earned, even though it has not been received.

3. d

No cash is involved because accrued revenue has been earned but not received.

4. d

Section 3
ACCRUED EXPENSES (ACCRUED LIABILITIES)

Introduction

Accrued expenses are expenses that have been incurred, but not yet paid for. To put it another way, an accrued expense is paid *after* being recorded on the books. Every adjusting entry for accrued expenses debits an expense account, increasing expenses on the income statement and reducing net income, and credits a payable account, increasing liabilities on the balance sheet.

How to Record Accrued Expenses

The general entry to record an accrued expense is:

[Various Titles] Expense   (income statement expense account)
    [Various Titles] Payable   (balance sheet liability account)
      To accrue _____ *expense*

Examples of Accrued Expenses

Accrued expenses include the following:

- Interest owed but not yet paid on borrowed funds.

    Interest Expense
      Interest Payable

- Rent owed, but not yet paid.

    Rent Expense
      Rent Payable

- Commissions and royalties owed but not yet paid.

    Commission [or Royalty] Expense
      Commission [or Royalty] Payable

- Utility and telephone bills owed, but not yet paid:

  Utilities [or Telephone] Expense
      Utilities [or Telephone] Payable

- Salary and wage expense owed, but not yet paid.

  Salaries Expense*
      Salaries Payable

  *Many companies use "Salaries Expense" for employees paid by the week and "Wages Expense" for employees paid by the hour.

- Property and other taxes owed, but not yet paid.

  Property [or Federal Income, State Income, etc.] Tax Expense
      Property [or Federal Income, State Income, etc.] Tax Payable

How Failure to Make the Adjustment Affects the Financial Statements

Failure to record an adjusting entry will have the following impacts on the financial statements:

- Liabilities will be understated on the balance sheet (because the omitted entry increases a liability account);

- Expenses will be understated on the income statement (because the entry increases an expense account); and, as a result,

- Net income will be overstated on the income statement.

Sample Problems

PROBLEM 1: GuCo pays sales reps a 5% commission on sales. GuCo had 20X5 sales of $500,000, but paid only $21,000 in commissions. How much does GuCo accrue in commissions on December 31?

SOLUTION 1: To compute: $500,000 sales for 20X5 x 5% = $25,000 commissions payable in 20X5. $25,000 payable – $21,000 actually paid = $4,000 accrued commissions. The adjusting journal entry is:

Commissions Expense	4,000	
Commissions Payable		4,000

To accrue 20X5 commissions

PROBLEM 2: On December 31, SuCo receives a $740 phone bill that it will pay the following month. What entry does SuCo record on December 31?

SOLUTION 2: On December 31, SuCo records the following adjusting entry:

Telephone Expense	740	
Telephone Payable		740

To accrue telephone expense

PROBLEM 3: RaCo pays employees weekly on Friday. But 20X7 ends on a Wednesday. If, for the last week of the year, gross payroll is $10,000, how much does RaCo accrue for salary expense?

SOLUTION 3: RaCo must accrue 20X7 salary expense for 3 of the 5 days, Monday, Tuesday, and Wednesday, which is 60% (3/5) of the week. To compute accrued payroll expense (payroll expense incurred but not paid) for the last week of 20X7: $10,000 x 60% = $6,000 accrued payroll expense for 20X7. (The remaining $4,000 of payroll expense for the week will be incurred in 20X8.)

RaCo's accrued payroll expense is recorded with an adjusting entry in the general journal as of the last day of the business year:

Salaries Expense	6,000	
Salaries Payable		6,000

To accrue salaries at year end

Without this entry, the company's 20X7 net income would be overstated because the expense would not have been recorded for 20X7. Also, 20X7 liabilities would be understated.

Accruing Interest Payable

Interest payable is accrued in the same way as interest receivable. On a short-term note, the interest accrues (builds up) and is usually paid along with the principal on the note's due date. On a long-term note, the interest is paid periodically, such as each month. If the accounting period ends before the interest is paid, interest expense is accrued on the last day of that period.

The formula to compute interest for a period is:

Face amount (principal) x annual interest rate x fraction of year = accrued interest

When a company gives a note to borrow money, the first entry is for the note:

Cash
    Note Payable
To record note payable

Subsequently, interest expense is accrued with the following entry:

Interest Expense
    Interest Payable
To accrue interest expense

PROBLEM 4: On November 1, 20X6, MiCo, which uses a calendar year, borrows $100,000 at 12% interest. How much interest expense should MiCo accrue as of December 31, 20X6, and how does it record the accrual on that day?

SOLUTION 4: To compute interest accrued as of December 31:

$100,000 principal x 12% annual interest = $12,000 x 2/12 (for November and December) = $2,000 accrued interest as of December 31. The adjusting entry in the general journal on December 31 is:

Interest Expense   2,000
    Interest Payable   2,000
To accrue 2 months' interest ($100,000 x 12% x 2/12)

The interest expense is recorded as of December 31 because the expense is incurred (owed, but not paid) as of the last day of the period.

Note that in all three problems, the adjusting entry increases an expense account, which reduces net income on the income statement, and increases a liability account, which increases liabilities on the balance sheet.

QUIZ 1   ACCRUED EXPENSES (ACCRUED LIABILITIES)

Problem I.

Make the following adjusting journal entries:

1. Accrue interest expense of $3,000

2. Accrue property tax expense of $1,200

3. Accrue salaries expense of $10,000

Problem II.

1. Your company has a 6-day workweek and payday is Saturday. Weekly salaries are $12,000, and your company contributes to each employee's pension by contributing 3% of salaries to the Pension Fund account. Make the adjusting journal entries when the accounting period ends on a Tuesday.

2. What adjusting entry (if any) do you record if the accounting period ends on a Saturday?

Problem III.

Your payroll for the last week of the year (your company uses a 5-day workweek) is $40,000 and December 31 falls on a Thursday. Record the adjusting journal entry at year end.

Problem IV.

Your company borrows $50,000 on a 6-month, 12% note on October 1. Year end is November 30. Record the accrued interest at November 30.

Problem V.

Multiple choice. Circle the correct answer.

1. What kind of account is Taxes Payable?

    a. asset
    b. liability
    c. revenue
    d. expense

2. If a company forgets to accrue utilities expense at year end, how does it affect net income?

    a. Net income will be overstated.
    b. Net income will be understated.
    c. Net income will be unaffected.

3. If a company fails to record an adjusting entry for property taxes, then net income will be . . .

    a. unaffected
    b. understated
    c. overstated
    d. understated or overstated depending on the amount

4. An accrued expense is one that is incurred but not yet paid.

    a. True   b. False

5. With an accrued expense, payment follows recognition of the expense.

    a. True   b. False

Problem VI.

Fill in the blanks.

1. An accrued expense is one that has been _____ but not _____.

2. An expense is accrued by debiting a(n) _____ account and crediting a(n) _____ account.

3. An adjusting entry to accrue an expense (increases/decreases) net income.

4. An expense recorded as incurred but not paid is presented as a(n) _____ on the balance sheet.

Problem VII.

Record the adjusting entries and any transaction entries on December 31 for each of the following:

1. On December 31, 20X1, FaCo incurs wage expense of $8,000 for December 29–31 that has not been either recorded or paid.

2. Rent for December of $2,300 will be paid on January 2.

3. Of the $1,000 in commissions payable on December 31, only $400 was paid.

QUIZ 1   Solutions and Explanations

Problem I.

1. Interest Expense   3,000
     Interest Payable   3,000
To accrue interest expense

2. Property Taxes   1,200
     Property Taxes Payable   1,200
To accrue property tax expense

3. Salaries Expense   10,000
     Salaries Payable   10,000
To accrue salaries expense

Problem II.

1. Salaries Expense   4,000*
     Salaries Payable   4,000
To accrue salaries expense

*$12,000 weekly payroll/6 days = $2,000 per day x 2 days (Monday and Tuesday) = $4,000

Pension Expense   120*
     Pension Payable   120
To accrue pension expense

*$4,000 accrued salaries expense x 3% pension contribution = $120 pension expense

2. If the workweek ends on a Saturday, the company will pay salaries for the entire week, so no salaries accrue (accrued expenses are expenses incurred *before* they are paid). Thus, no adjusting entry is recorded; only an ordinary transaction entry is needed. However, pension contributions might accrue depending on the rules of the particular plan.

Problem III.

Wages (or Salaries) Expense	32,000*	
Wages (or Salaries) Payable		32,000

To accrue wages (or salaries)

*$40,000 payroll x 4/5 of the week (Monday–Thursday) = $32,000 payroll expense accrued for the week.

Problem IV.

Interest Expense	1,000	
Interest Payable		1,000

To accrue 2 months' interest expense ($50,000 x 12% x 2/12)

Problem V.

1. b
A payable account is a liability.

2. a
When a company does not record an expense, expenses are understated (too low) on the income statement, and net income is overstated (too high).

3. c
Because not all expenses are on the books, net income will be overstated.

4. a

5. a

Problem VI.

1. incurred, paid

2. expense, payable (or liability)

3. decreases

4. liability

Problem VII.

On December 31, 20X1, FaCo records the following adjusting entries:

1. $8,000 in accrued wages (stated in the data) have been accrued:

Wages Expense	8,000	
Wages Payable		8,000

To accrue wages expense

2. $2,300 in accrued rent:

Rent Expense	2,300	
Rent Payable		2,300

To accrue rent expense

3. There is a transaction entry for the commissions paid:

Commissions Expense	400	
Cash		400

There is an adjusting entry for accrued commissions:

Commissions Expense	600*	
Commissions Payable		600

To accrue commissions expense

*$1,000 commissions owed – $400 paid = $600 accrued.

QUIZ 2   ACCRUED EXPENSES (ACCRUED LIABILITIES)

Problem I.

Make the following adjusting journal entries:

1. Accrue interest expense of $8,000

2. Accrue utility expense of $2,500

3. Accrue sales commissions of $18,000

4. Accrue salaries expense of $42,000

Problem II.

Your company has a 5-day workweek and pays employees on Friday. The weekly gross payroll is $100,000, and the year ends on Thursday. Record the adjusting journal entry at year end.

Problem III.

Multiple choice. Circle the correct answer.

1. Accrued taxes appear on the balance sheet as a liability.

    a. True   b. False

2. A company failed to accrue employee salary expense. What effect does this have on net income and liabilities, respectively?

    a. overstates net income but does not affect liabilities
    b. overstates net income and understates liabilities
    c. understates net income and overstates liabilities
    d. understates net income but does not affect liabilities

3. An accrued expense is paid when incurred.

    a. True   b. False

4. An adjusting entry to accrue interest expense does not involve a cash payment.

a. True   b. False

Problem IV.

On December 1, 20X3, WyCo, a calendar year company, borrows $30,000 on a 6-month, 8% note payable. The interest is payable at the maturity date. Of the amount borrowed, $6,000 will be used to pay WyCo's 20X3 income tax when it files a return in 20X4. Another portion of the loan will go to pay part of WyCo's weekly payroll of $12,000 for the last week of the year. WyCo uses a 5-day workweek and payday is Friday. What adjusting entries does WyCo record on Tuesday, December 31, 20X3?

QUIZ 2   Solutions and Explanations

Problem I.

1. Interest Expense   8,000
    Interest Payable   8,000
To accrue interest expense

2. Utilities Expense   2,500
    Utilities Payable   2,500
To accrue utilities expense

3. Sales Commissions Expense   18,000
    Sales Commissions Payable   18,000
To accrue sales commissions

4. Salaries Expense   42,000
    Salaries Payable   42,000
To accrue salaries expense

Problem II.

Salaries Expense   80,000*
    Salaries Payable   80,000
To accrue salaries expense (Mon.-Thurs.)

*Your company must accrue salaries for 4 of 5 workdays (Monday–Thursday) or 80% of the week. To compute: $100,000 x 80% = $80,000

Problem III.

1. a
When taxes accrue, a liability account (Taxes Payable) is credited, increasing liabilities on the balance sheet.

2. b
Net income is overstated because total expenses are understated (lower than they should be). Liabilities are also understated because the appropriate liability account was not increased.

3. b
Accrued means that the expense was incurred *before* it was paid.

4. a

The entry debits an expense account and credits a liability account; no cash is involved.

Problem IV.

First, decide what adjusting entries there are. According to the data, there are three adjusting entries:

1. Accrued interest on the loan. To compute: $30,000 face amount x 8% annual interest = $2,400 x 1/12 (for the month of December) = $200 accrued interest.

Interest Expense	200	
Interest Payable		200
To accrue interest expense		

2. There is accrued income tax, an expense that WyCo incurred in 20X3 but will not pay until 20X4.

Income Tax Expense	6,000	
Income Tax Payable		6,000
To accrue income tax expense		

3. Wyco must accrue 2 days' salary for Monday and Tuesday of the last week of the year. To compute: $12,000 weekly payroll x 2/5 (Monday and Tuesday) = $4,800 accrued salary expense.

Salaries Expense	4,800	
Salaries Payable		4,800
To accrue salaries expense		

Section 4
REVENUE COLLECTED IN ADVANCE (UNEARNED REVENUE)

Introduction

Unearned revenue (sometimes referred to as deferred revenue) results from the receipt of payment for services not yet performed. When cash is collected in advance, the business incurs a liability for work to be performed, services to be rendered, or goods to be delivered. In accrual basis accounting, a payment received in advance is not recognized as revenue. Only after the revenue is *earned* can the business recognize it. That is why unearned revenue is also referred to as *deferred revenue*.

How to Record Unearned Revenue

Unearned revenue involves both a transaction entry and an adjusting entry. The original transaction entry is made when the cash is received. The adjusting entry is made at the end of the year (or other period). There are two ways to record the receipt of cash before the revenue is earned:

1a. The first way is to debit Cash and set up a liability account that may have a number of titles including Unearned Revenue, Revenue Collected In Advance, Revenue Received In Advance, and so on. The transaction entry to record the revenue collected in advance is as follows:

Cash   (balance sheet asset account)
    Unearned Revenue   (balance sheet liability account)
To record revenue received in advance

1b. The adjusting entry at the end of the period simply transfers the amount earned (recognized) from the balance sheet account to the income statement account as follows:

Unearned Revenue   (balance sheet account)
    Revenue   (income statement account)
To recognize revenue earned for the period

2a. The second way to record revenue collected in advance is to debit Cash and credit Revenue. The transaction entry to record the revenue collected in advance is as follows:

Cash   (balance sheet account)
    Revenue   (income statement account)
To record revenue received in advance

2b. The adjusting entry recorded at the end of the period reduces the balance in the Revenue account to the amount actually earned for the period. The unearned portion is transferred to Unearned Revenue (this account may have to be set up when the adjusting entry is made), where it is held until earned in the future.

Revenue   (income statement account)
    Unearned Revenue   (balance sheet account)
To reduce the balance in Revenue and defer unearned revenue

The ending balance in the Revenue and Unearned Revenue accounts is the same, regardless of which account was initially credited.

Examples of Unearned Revenue

Examples of revenues received in advance include:

- Advances on legal, accounting, programming, consulting or other services.

Original entry	Adjusting entry
Cash	Unearned Revenue
Unearned Revenue	Revenue

or

Cash	Revenue
Revenue	Unearned Revenue

- Commissions and royalties received in advance.

Original entry	Adjusting entry
Cash	Unearned Commission [or Royalty] Revenue
Unearned Commission [or Royalty]	Commission [or Royalty] Revenue

or

Original entry	Adjusting entry
Cash	Commission [or Royalty] Revenue
Commission [Or Royalty] Revenue	Unearned Commission [Or Royalty] Revenue

- Rent received in advance.

Original entry	Adjusting entry
Cash	Unearned Rent Revenue
Unearned Rent Revenue	Rent Revenue

or

Cash	Rent Revenue
Rent Revenue	Unearned Rent Revenue

- Interest revenue received in advance (such as an advance of the first month's interest on a loan).

Original entry	Adjusting entry
Cash	Unearned Interest Revenue
Unearned Interest Revenue	Interest Revenue

or

Cash	Interest Revenue
Interest Revenue	Unearned Interest Revenue

How Failure to Record the Adjustment Affects the Financial Statements

If the original entry is to Unearned Revenue, failure to record an adjusting entry will have the following impacts on the financial statements:

- Liabilities will be overstated on the balance sheet (because the omitted adjusting entry would have reduced the liability account);

- Revenues will be understated on the income statement (because the omitted adjusting entry would have increased a revenue account); and, as a result,

- Net income will be understated on the income statement.

If the original entry is to Revenue, failure to record an adjusting entry will have the opposite effects on the financial statements:

- Liabilities will be understated on the balance sheet (because the omitted adjusting entry would have increased a liability account);

- Revenues will be overstated on the income statement (because the omitted adjusting entry would have decreased a revenue account); and, as a result,

- Net income will be overstated on the income statement.

Sample Problems

The following problems involve an initial transaction entry that records the receipt of cash, and an adjusting entry to recognize the amount of revenue earned for the period. In Problem 1A, an unearned revenue account is credited in the transaction entry; in Problem 1B, a revenue account is credited in the transaction entry.

> **PROBLEM 1A:** Renovation, Inc. signs a $50,000 painting contract with CriCo and receives a $20,000 advance. When Renovation's year ends, it has completed 10% of the job. What entry is recorded upon receipt of the cash? What adjusting entry is made at year end?

SOLUTION 1A: The original entry records the receipt of cash:

Cash	20,000	
Unearned Painting Revenue*		20,000
To record cash advance on CriCo job		

*This account may also be called Painting Revenue Collected In Advance or Painting Revenue Received In Advance.

Before you can record the adjusting entry at year end, you must compute the amount earned. According to the data, this is a $50,000 job, and Renovation has completed 10% of it. To compute: $50,000 job x 10% completed = $5,000 earned.

Unearned Painting Revenue	5,000	
Painting Revenue		5,000
To record revenue earned		

The debit to Unearned Painting Revenue reduces liabilities by the amount earned and leaves in this account a balance of $15,000 (the amount of revenue that has *not* been earned). The credit to Painting Revenue recognizes $5,000 as income.

This can be illustrated with T-accounts, where "a" indicates the original transaction entry and "b" indicates the adjusting entry.

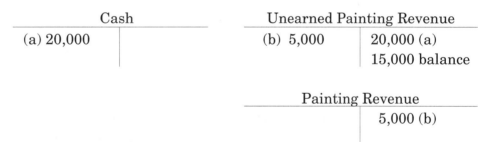

PROBLEM 1B: Use the facts from Problem 1A, but this time credit collection of the cash advance to Revenue in the initial entry. What entry is recorded upon receipt of the cash? What adjusting entry is made at year end?

SOLUTION 1B: The original entry is:

Cash	20,000	
Painting Revenue		20,000
To record cash advance on CriCo job		

The debit to Cash, an asset account, increases that account balance by $20,000, and the credit to Painting Revenue increases the balance in that account by $20,000 even though no revenue has been earned. Unless the entire $20,000 revenue is earned during the period, the balance in Painting Revenue will have to be reduced.

The adjusting entry at year end is:

Painting Revenue	15,000	
Unearned Painting Revenue		15,000

To correct Revenue balance to amount earned

To compute the amount of revenue earned: $50,000 job x 10% completed = $5,000 earned. The debit to Painting Revenue reduces the balance to the $5,000 earned during the year ($20,000 balance – $15,000 unearned = $5,000 balance actually earned). The credit to Unearned Painting Revenue leaves an ending balance in that account of $15,000 (the amount of the advance still to be earned).

This can be illustrated with T-accounts where "a" indicates the original transaction entry and "b" indicates the adjusting entry.

Cash		Unearned Painting Revenue	
(a) 20,000			15,000 (b)

	Painting Revenue	
(b) 15,000	20,000 (a)	
	5,000 balance	

Although the entries in Problems 1A and 1B are different, both lead to the same result: an ending balance in Painting Revenue of $5,000 and an ending balance in Unearned Painting Revenue of $15,000.

PROBLEM 2: On May 1, your company collects a cash advance of $24,000 for 1 year's rent. Your company's year ends December 31. What two possible sets of entries, original and adjusting, can be used to record collection of the cash advance and recognition of the rent earned as of year end?

SOLUTION 2: One set of entries begins with a transaction entry that records the advance payment in Unearned Rent Revenue:

<u>May 1 (original transaction entry)</u>:
Cash	24,000	
Unearned Rent Revenue*		24,000

To record rent advance

*This account may also be called Rent Collected In Advance.

The credit to Unearned Rent Revenue creates a liability of $24,000.

On December 31, your company records an adjusting entry that recognizes $16,000 in rent revenue ($24,000 x 8/12 for May–December = $16,000 earned revenue).

<u>Dec. 31 (adjusting entry)</u>
Unearned Rent Revenue	16,000	
Rent Revenue		16,000

To record rent earned

The debit to Unearned Rent Revenue reduces the liability by the $16,000 earned, leaving a balance of $8,000 to be earned in future months. The credit to Rent Revenue recognizes the $16,000 earned as of December 31.

A second set of entries begins with a transaction entry that records collection of the advance payment in Rent Revenue:

<u>May 1 (original transaction entry)</u>:
Cash	24,000	
Rent Revenue		24,000

To record rent advance

The credit to Rent Revenue increases the account balance by $24,000. Unless the company earns the full $24,000 by year end, it will have to reduce the Rent Revenue to the amount that is earned.

On December 31, you compute only $16,000 in rent revenue earned during the year: $24,000 x 8/12 for May–December = $16,000. What amount must you remove from the Rent Revenue balance to leave only the $16,000 earned? To compute: $24,000 current balance – $16,000 ending balance = $8,000 that must be removed from Rent Revenue.

Dec. 31 (adjusting entry)

Rent Revenue	8,000	
Unearned Rent Revenue		8,000

To record rent revenue earned

The debit to Rent Revenue reduces this account by $8,000, leaving a balance of $16,000, the amount actually earned ($24,000 balance – $8,000 reduction = $16,000 earned as of December 31). The credit to Unearned Rent Revenue creates a liability of $8,000 for the revenue that your company will earn in future months.

Both sets of entries result in the same year-end account balances: $16,000 in Rent Revenue, to recognize the amount earned during the year, and $8,000 in Unearned Rent Revenue that your company must earn in the future.

QUIZ 1   REVENUE COLLECTED IN ADVANCE (UNEARNED REVENUE)

Problem I.

Prepare the adjusting journal entry for each situation:

1. You collect a $12,000 advance for 1 year's rent and credit Rent Revenue. At year end, 3 months have elapsed.

2. You collect a $12,000 advance for 1 year's rent and credit Unearned Rent Revenue. At year end, 3 months have elapsed.

3. Your company collects a $20,000 advance for a $100,000 order to produce widgets and credits Revenue. At year end, your company has completed 12% of the job.

4. Your company collects a $20,000 advance for a $100,000 job and credits Unearned Revenue. At year end, your company has completed 12% of the job.

Problem II.

Your firm signs a contract to sell Widget, Inc. products for a 20% commission on sales. During the year, Widget pays your firm $7,000 in commissions, which you credit to Unearned Commission Revenue. By year end, your firm achieves $25,000 in sales. What adjusting entry do you record on December 31?

Problem III.

On May 15, your company accepts a $28,000 advance on a 2-year, $70,000 painting job. On December 31, management tells you that it has completed 30% of the work. What original transaction entry do you record on May 15 if the amount received is recorded as revenue? What adjusting entry do you record at year end?

Problem IV.

Fill in the blanks.

1. Three possible names for a revenue liability account are _____ _____ and _____. (Answers may be more than one word.)

2. Unearned revenue appears on a balance sheet as a(n) _____.

3. Revenue is recorded when _____.

4. For cash collected in advance, debit _____ and credit _____.

Problem V.

Multiple choice. Circle the correct answer.

1. If you collect 3 months' rent on December 1 and your year ends December 31, the revenue earned will be less than the cash collected.

    a. True   b. False

2. A company collects cash in advance for a job and credits Revenue. It earns part of the advance by completing work during the year. If it omits the proper adjusting entry at year end, liabilities will be . . .

    a. understated
    b. overstated
    c. unaffected

3. A company collects cash in advance for a job, credits Deferred Revenue, then completes part of the work. If it fails to record an adjusting entry at year end, liabilities will be . . .

    a. understated
    b. overstated
    c. unaffected

Problem VI.

Match the transaction entry in Column A with the adjusting entry in Column B.

<u>A</u>

1. Cash
   Revenue
2. Cash
   Unearned Revenue

<u>B</u>

1. Revenue
   Unearned Revenue
2. Unearned Revenue
   Revenue

QUIZ 1   Solutions and Explanations

Problem I.

1. Rent Revenue   9,000
     Unearned Rent Revenue   9,000
To record unearned revenue ($12,000 – $3,000 earned)

2. Unearned Rent Revenue   3,000
     Rent Revenue   3,000
To record revenue earned ($1,000/month x 3 months)

3. Revenue   8,000
     Unearned Revenue   8,000
To record unearned revenue ($20,000 – [$100,000 x 12%])

To compute the amount of revenue recognized, multiply the portion of the job completed by the *total job cost, not* the amount of the advance: $100,000 job x 12% completed = $12,000 in revenue recognized. By how much will the balance in the Revenue account have to be reduced to leave a year-end balance of $12,000? To compute: $20,000 advance – $12,000 required ending balance = $8,000 reduction. The entry above reduced the balance in Revenue by $8,000, leaving an ending balance of $12,000, the amount of income that your company can recognize for the year.

4. Unearned revenue   12,000
     Revenue   12,000
To record revenue earned ($100,000 x 12%)

The amount of revenue recognized depends on the percentage of the $100,000 job completed—*not* on the $20,000 advance. To compute: $100,000 job x 12% completed = $12,000 in revenue earned.

Problem II.

Unearned Commission Revenue	5,000	
Commission Revenue		5,000

To record revenue earned ($25,000 x 20%)

Only the $5,000 earned can be recognized as revenue at year end.

Problem III.

Original entry on May 15:

Cash	28,000	
Painting Revenue		28,000

To record revenue

Adjusting entry at year end:

Painting Revenue	7,000	
Unearned Painting Revenue		7,000

To reduce Revenue to amount earned

To record the adjusting entry, you must compute the amount earned: $70,000 job x 30% completed = $21,000 earned (your company completed 30% of the $70,000 earned, *not* 30% of the advance). The Revenue account must show an ending balance of $21,000. To compute: $28,000 credited to Revenue in the original entry – $21,000 required ending balance = $7,000 reduction.

Problem IV.

1. Unearned Revenue, Revenue Collected In Advance, Revenue Received In Advance, Deferred Revenue

2. liability

3. earned

4. Cash, Revenue *or* Unearned Revenue *or* Deferred Revenue

Problem V.

1. a

Revenue earned is one-third of cash collected.

2. a

Unearned revenue, a liability, is not recorded.

3. b

Revenue earned is not recorded.

Problem VI.

1. 1 and 1

2. 2 and 2

QUIZ 2   REVENUE COLLECTED IN ADVANCE (UNEARNED REVENUE)

Problem I.

Prepare the adjusting journal entry for each situation:

1. You collect a $24,000 advance for 1 year's rent and credit Rent Revenue. Your company's year ends 3 months later.

2. You collect $24,000 in advance for 1 year's rent and credit Rent Revenue Collected In Advance. Your company's year ends 3 months later.

3. You collect $25,000 in advance for a $100,000 advertising order and credit Advertising Revenue. You complete 15% of the job before your company's year ends.

4. You collect $25,000 in advance for a $100,000 advertising order and credit Unearned Advertising Revenue. You complete 15% of the job before your company's year ends.

Problem II.

Your company signs a 2-year contract to sell MiCo's products for a 20% commission on sales. During the year, MiCo remits $7,000 to your firm for commissions that you credit to Commission Revenue. At year end your company has achieved sales of $35,000 from MiCo's products this year. What adjusting entry do you record on December 31?

Problem III.

Your company undertakes a $27,000 painting job and receives an advance of $10,000, which you credit to Painting Revenue. At year end your firm has completed 1/3 of the work. What adjusting entry do you record?

Problem IV.

Fill in the blanks.

1. If the original transaction entry records revenue collected in advance in the Revenue account and the company earns only part of the revenue by year end, the adjusting entry at year end will (increase/reduce) _____ the balance in Revenue.

2. Unearned revenue is the result of revenue collected _____ (before/after) it is earned.

3. Revenue is booked when _____, not when _____.

4. Unearned revenue appears as a(n) _____ on the balance sheet.

5. Payment received in advance is debited to _____ and credited to either _____ or _____.

Problem V.

Multiple choice. Circle the correct answer.

1. You collect $10,000 during the year and credit Revenue. If you earn all $10,000, you need no adjusting entry at year end.

    a. True   b. False

2. When revenue is received in advance and part of it is earned by the end of the period, the adjusting entry affects both the income statement *and* balance sheet.

    a. True   b. False

3. If a company collects cash in advance for a job and credits Revenue, then completes part of the work but fails to record an adjusting entry at year end, net income is . . .

    a. understated
    b. overstated
    c. unaffected

4. If a company collects cash in advance for a job and credits Deferred Revenue, then completes part of the work but fails to record an adjusting entry at year end, net income is . . .

    a. understated
    b. overstated
    c. unaffected

5. If a company collects cash in advance and credits Deferred Revenue, the adjusting entry at year end is a debit to. . .

    a. Revenue
    b. Deferred Revenue
    c. Cash

QUIZ 2 Solutions and Explanations

Problem I.

1. Rent Revenue   18,000
        Unearned Rent Revenue   18,000
To record unearned revenue

Although the $24,000 advance payment was credited to Rent Revenue, only $6,000 was earned by year end. To compute: $24,000 rent for 1 year x 3/12 year elapsed = $6,000 rent revenue earned. Therefore, at year end, the balance in the Rent Revenue account must be reduced to $6,000. To compute: $24,000 current balance – $6,000 required ending balance = $18,000 reduction. The $18,000 is transferred to Unearned Rent Revenue, a liability account, to be earned in the future.

2. Rent Revenue Collected In Advance   6,000
        Rent Revenue   6,000
To record revenue earned

The entire $24,000 advance was credited to the liability account, Rent Revenue Collected In Advance (Unearned Rent Revenue is another name for the account). At year end, the $6,000 earned ($24,000 advance x 3/12 for the 3 months elapsed) is transferred to Rent Revenue to recognize the income.

3. Advertising Revenue   10,000
        Unearned Advertising Revenue   10,000
To record unearned revenue

The $25,000 advance was credited to Advertising Revenue, but by year end, only $15,000 has been earned. To compute: $100,000 job x 15% of job completed = $15,000 earned as of year end. This means that at year end, the balance in Advertising Revenue must be reduced to $15,000. To compute: $25,000 current balance – $15,000 required ending balance = $10, 000 reduction. The $10,000 is transferred to Unearned Advertising Revenue (Deferred Advertising Revenue is also correct) to be earned in the future.

4. Unearned Advertising Revenue   15,000
     Advertising Revenue   15,000
To record revenue earned

The $25,000 advance was originally credited to the liability account, Unearned Advertising Revenue. By year end, your company has earned $15,000 ($100,000 job x 15% of job completed), so you must both reduce liabilities by this amount and recognize that this amount has been earned by increasing the balance in Advertising Revenue. Both goals are accomplished by the adjusting entry above.

Problem II.

The company does not record any adjusting entry because the ending balance in Commission Revenue is correct. To compute: $35,000 order x 20% commission = $7,000 earned. This is the amount originally credited to Commission Revenue, so no adjusting entry is required.

Problem III.

Painting Revenue   1,000
     Unearned Painting Revenue   1,000
To reduce Revenue to the required balance ($10,000 – $9,000)

To compute the amount earned as of year end: $27,000 job x 33% of work completed = $9,000 earned. Thus the balance in Painting Revenue must be reduced to $9,000. To compute: $10,000 current balance in Painting Revenue from original entry – $9,000 ending balance = $1,000 required reduction. The account Unearned Painting Revenue is set up for the $1,000 remaining portion of the advance to be earned in the future.

Problem IV.

1. reduce

2. before

3. earned, collected (or received)

4. liability

5. Cash, Revenue, Deferred Revenue (Unearned Revenue is also correct)

Problem V.

1. a

    All revenue received has been earned, so the accounts do not need to be adjusted.

2. a

    The adjusting entry affects Revenue, an income statement account, and unearned revenue affects Deferred Revenue (Unearned Revenue), a balance sheet account.

3. b

    Because not all of the credit to Revenue in the original entry has been earned, the balance in Revenue should be reduced at year end by an adjusting entry. If an adjusting entry is not reduced, then revenue is overstated and net income is overstated.

4. a

    Unearned Revenue is a liability account. At year end, the balance must be reduced by the amount earned, which is transferred to Revenue. If Revenue is not credited with the amount earned, then revenue will be understated, and so will net income.

5. b

    The balance in Deferred Revenue must be decreased by the amount earned, and Revenue must be increased by the same amount to recognize the income. The Cash account is not used in adjusting entries.

Section 5
PREPAID (DEFERRED) EXPENSES

Introduction

Prepaid (or deferred) expenses are those paid before the expense is incurred (that is, before the goods are used or the service is performed). When an expense is paid in advance, the amount is recorded in an asset account such as Prepaid Office Supplies, Prepaid Insurance, or Prepaid Rent. As the goods are used or the service is performed, the asset account is reduced and the corresponding expense account is increased.

In accrual basis accounting, a prepayment cannot be recognized as an expense. Only after the expense has been incurred can the business recognize the expense.

How to Record Prepayments and Adjustments

Prepaid (or deferred) expenses involve both a transaction entry and an adjusting entry. The original transaction entry is made when cash is paid. The adjusting entry is made at the end of the year (or other period). There are two ways to record payment of an expense:

1a. The first way is to debit an asset account known as a prepaid expense account and to credit Cash. The prepaid expense account title will describe the type of prepaid expense involved, such as Prepaid Rent, Prepaid Interest or Prepaid Office Supplies. The transaction entry to record a prepaid or deferred expense is as follows:

> Prepaid [Various Titles]   (balance sheet asset account)
>   Cash   (balance sheet asset account)
> *To record prepayment of [various] expense*

Note that this method of recording the *transaction* entry involves two balance sheet accounts. *Adjusting* entries involve a balance sheet account and an income statement account.

1b. The adjusting entry at the end of the period simply transfers the amount of the expense that has been recognized (used up) from the asset account to the expense account:

    [Various] Expense   (income statement account)
        Prepaid [Various]   (balance sheet account)
    To recognize [various] expense

2a. The second way to record the advance payment of an expense is to debit the appropriate expense account and credit Cash. The transaction entry to record advance payment of an expense in this way is as follows:

    [Various] Expense   (income statement account)
        Cash   (balance sheet account)
    To record prepayment of [various] expense

2b. The adjusting entry recorded at the end of the period reduces the balance in the expense account to the amount of the expense incurred during the period. The unused portion is transferred to a prepaid account (which may have to be set up when the adjusting entry is made), where it is held until the expense is incurred in the future.

    Prepaid [Various]   (balance sheet account)
        [Various] Expense   (income statement account)
    To reduce the balance in [various] expense and defer the unused portion

Regardless of which method is used initially to record the transaction entry, the adjusting entry recognizes the portion of the expense that was used up during the period and defers the unused portion until it is used up in the future.

Examples of Prepaid Expenses

Examples of prepaid expenses include:

- Prepaid insurance.

    <u>Original entry</u>   <u>Adjusting entry</u>
    Prepaid Insurance   Insurance Expense
        Cash   Prepaid Insurance

or

    Insurance Expense   Prepaid Insurance
        Cash   Insurance Expense

- Supplies on hand (that is, office or other supplies used from day to day, *not* an inventory of supplies that are sold to customers as-is or processed and then sold).

Original entry	Adjusting entry
Prepaid Supplies*	Supplies Expense
Cash	Prepaid Supplies

*This account is often referred to as Supplies On Hand.

or

Supplies Expense	Prepaid Supplies
Cash	Supplies Expense

- Rent paid in advance.

Original entry	Adjusting entry
Prepaid Rent	Rent Expense
Cash	Prepaid Rent

or

Rent Expense	Prepaid Rent
Cash	Rent Expense

- Legal Fees (or other fees).

Original entry	Adjusting entry
Prepaid Legal Fees	Legal Expense
Cash	Prepaid Legal Fees

or

Legal Expense	Prepaid Legal Fees
Cash	Legal Expense

- Advance payments for painting (or other) services.

Original entry	Adjusting entry

Prepaid Painting Expense
   (or Painting Advance)
     Cash
	Painting Expense
	   Prepaid Painting Expense
	     (or Painting Advance)

or

Painting Expense
   Cash
	Prepaid Painting Expense
	   (or Painting Advance)
	     Painting Expense

How Failure to Record the Adjustment Affects the Financial Statements

If the original entry is to a *prepaid* account, failure to record an adjusting entry will affect the financial statements as follows:

- Assets will be overstated on the balance sheet (because the omitted adjusting entry would have reduced an asset account);

- Expenses will be understated on the income statement (because the omitted adjusting entry would have increased an expense account); and, as a result,

- Net income will be overstated on the income statement.

If the original entry is to an *expense* account, failure to record an adjusting entry will have the opposite effects on the financial statements:

- Assets will be understated on the balance sheet (because the omitted adjusting entry would have increased an asset account);

- Expenses will be overstated on the income statement (because the omitted adjusting entry would have decreased an expense account; and, as a result,

- Net income will be understated on the income statement.

Sample Problems

PROBLEM 1A: On October 1, 20X2, CraCo, a calendar year company, prepays a 1-year insurance premium of $30,000 and records the payment in Prepaid Insurance. What entry does CraCo record on October 1? What entry does CraCo record at year end?

SOLUTION 1A: CraCo records the following transaction entry on October 1:

Prepaid Insurance	30,000	
Cash		30,000

To record prepayment of 1-year premium

Cash is credited because cash is being paid. The asset account Prepaid Insurance (or Unexpired Insurance) is debited to increase that account by the same amount.

The adjusting entry at year end is:

Insurance Expense	7,500*	
Prepaid Insurance		7,500

To record insurance Oct.–Dec. expense ($30,000 x 3/12)

*$30,000/12 months = $2,500 per month x 3 months (October, November, December) = $7,500 insurance expense used up by year end.

At year end, the adjusting entry debits Insurance Expense, increasing that account by $7,500 to recognize insurance used up.

The entry credits Prepaid Insurance, reducing that account by the same amount, leaving a balance of $22,500 ($30,000 – $7,500).

To illustrate with T-accounts, where "a" indicates the original transaction entry and "b" indicates the adjusting entry:

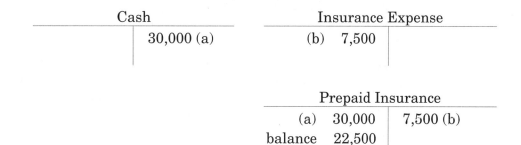

PROBLEM 1B: Assume the same facts as in Problem 1A except that CraCo records the $30,000 payment in Insurance Expense. What entry does Craco record on October 1? What entry does CraCo record at year end?

SOLUTION 1B: CraCo records the following transaction entry on October 1:

Insurance Expense	30,000	
Cash		30,000

To record prepayment of 1-year premium

Cash is credited because cash is paid, and the entire prepayment is recorded in the expense account.

The adjusting entry at year end is:

Prepaid Insurance	22,500	
Insurance Expense		22,500

To adjust insurance expense

To compute the amount of insurance that CraCo has used up: $30,000/12 months = $2,500 per month x 3 months (October, November, December) = $7,500 insurance expense used up by year end. The credit to Insurance Expense reduces the balance to the $7,500 used up during the year ($30,000 balance – $22,500 to be used in future months). The debit to Prepaid Insurance (this account may have to be set up when the adjusting entry is made) leaves a balance in that account of $22,500.

This can be illustrated with T-accounts, where "a" indicates the original transaction entry and "b" indicates the adjusting entry:

Cash		Prepaid Insurance	
	30,000 (a)	(b) 22,500	

Insurance Expense	
(a) 30,000	22,500 (b)
balance 7,500	

The transaction and adjusting entries in Problems 1A and 1B both lead to an ending balance in Insurance Expense of $7,500 and an ending balance in Prepaid Insurance of $22,500.

PROBLEM 2A: During the year, your firm buys $18,000 in office supplies and records the entire prepayment in Supplies On Hand. At year end, you have $4,000 of supplies on hand. Record the transaction and adjusting entries.

SOLUTION 2A:

<u>Transaction entry using Supplies On Hand</u>

Supplies On Hand*	18,000	
Cash		18,000

To record supplies purchase
*This account may also be called Prepaid Supplies.

<u>Adjusting entry</u>

Supplies Expense	14,000	
Supplies On Hand		14,000

To record supplies expense

The debit to Supplies Expense recognizes the $14,000 of supplies used up as of year end. The credit to Supplies On Hand reduces the asset by the $14,000 of office supplies that were used up.

To illustrate with T-accounts where "a" indicates the original transaction entry and "b" indicates the adjusting entry:

Cash		Supplies Expense	
	18,000 (a)	(b) 14,000	

Supplies On Hand		
(a) 18,000	14,000 (b)	
balance 4,000		

PROBLEM 2B: As in Problem 2A, your firm buys $18,000 in office supplies but this time records the entire prepayment to Supplies Expense. At year end, you have $4,000 of supplies on hand. Record the transaction and adjusting entries.

SOLUTION 2B:

<u>Transaction entry using Supplies Expense</u>

Supplies Expense	18,000	
Cash		18,000

To record supplies purchase

<u>Adjusting entry</u>

Supplies On Hand	4,000	
Supplies Expense		4,000

To adjust supplies expense

The credit to Supplies expense is the amount that must be removed from this account so that the ending balance reflects only the supplies used up during the year.

The debit to Supplies On Hand (which may have to be set up for you to record the adjusting entry) leaves the $4,000 in supplies that will be used up in the future.

To illustrate with T-accounts, where "a" indicates the original transaction entry and "b" indicates the adjusting entry:

Cash		Supplies On Hand	
	18,000 (a)	(b) 4,000	

	Supplies Expense	
(a) 18,000	4,000 (b)	
balance 14,000		

Note that both sets of entries (Solutions 2A and 2B) leave an ending balance in Supplies Expense of $14,000 and an ending balance in Supplies On Hand of $4,000.

QUIZ 1   PREPAID (DEFERRED) EXPENSES

Problem I.

For each of the following, record the adjusting entry:

1. Your company prepays $12,000 rent for 1 year and debits Rent Expense. Your company's year ends 4 months later.

2. Your company prepays $12,000 of rent for 1 year and debits Prepaid Rent. Your company's year ends 4 months later.

3. Your company buys $30,000 of office supplies and debits Supplies On Hand. At year end there are $9,000 of supplies on hand (unused).

4. Your company buys $30,000 of office supplies and debits Supplies Expense. At year end, there are $9,000 of supplies on hand (unused).

Problem II.

You give PaintCo a $12,000 advance on a $100,000 paint job and record it in Painting Advance (prepaid painting expense). By year end, PaintCo has completed 10% of the job. Record the adjusting entry.

Problem III.

You prepay $24,000 for 2 years of insurance premiums and debit Unexpired Insurance (prepaid insurance expense). Your company's year ends 4 months later. Make the adjusting entry.

Problem IV.

Fill in the blanks.

1. Unexpired Insurance is a(n) _____ account.

2. Supplies On Hand is a(n) _____ account.

3. A prepaid expense involves payment of cash _____ the expense is incurred.

4. An expense should be recorded when it has been _____ .

5. If you prepay insurance and debit Insurance Expense, then use up only part of the insurance before year end, the year-end adjusting entry will (reduce/increase) _____ the balance in Insurance Expense.

Problem V.

Multiple choice. Circle the correct answer.

1. You prepay rent and debit Rent Expense. If you do not record the adjusting entry at the end of the period, total assets on the balance sheet will be . . .

    a. understated
    b. overstated
    c. unaffected

2. You prepay rent and debit Prepaid Rent. If you do not record the adjusting entry at the end of the period, total assets on the balance sheet will be . . .

    a. understated
    b. overstated
    c. unaffected

3. Your company buys office supplies and debits Supplies On Hand for $50,000. At year end, you estimate that $8,000 of supplies are on hand. The adjusting entry will leave an ending balance in Supplies Expense of _____ and an ending balance in Supplies On Hand of _____.

   a. $50,000 and zero
   b. zero and $50,000
   c. $8,000 and $42,000
   d. $42,000 and $8,000

4. If the entry to record a prepaid insurance premium is a debit to Prepaid Insurance, then the *adjusting* entry to reflect insurance expense at year end is a debit to . . .

   a. Insurance Expense
   b. Unexpired Insurance
   c. Cash

5. Regardless of which transaction entry is made, an adjusting entry affects both the income statement and the balance sheet.

   a. True   b. False

QUIZ 1 Solutions and Explanations

Problem I.

1. Prepaid Rent   8,000
       Rent Expense   8,000
To recognize rent expense ($12,000 – $4,000)

The original entry debited Rent Expense for the entire $12,000 prepayment. However, by year end, your company had used up (incurred) only 4 months' rent. Thus, the ending balance in Rent Expense must be $4,000 (4/12 x $12,000). To achieve this balance, you must reduce (credit) the balance in Rent Expense by $8,000. To compute: $12,000 prepayment – $4,000 required ending balance = $8,000 reduction. The $8,000 is transferred to Prepaid Rent (an account that may have to be established just for this entry), where it will be held until used in the future.

2. Rent Expense   4,000
       Prepaid Rent   4,000
To recognize rent expense ($1,000/month x 4 months)

The original entry debited Prepaid Rent for the entire $12,000 prepayment. At year end, the $4,000 (4/12 x $12,000) in rent used up must be transferred to Rent Expense.

3. Supplies Expense   21,000
       Supplies On Hand   21,000
To record supplies expense ($30,000 – $9,000)

The original entry debited Supplies On Hand for the entire $30,000 prepayment. At year end, the $21,000 must be transferred to Supplies Expense. The remainder stays in Supplies On Hand, another name for a prepaid supplies account, until it is used up in the future.

To illustrate with T-accounts, where "a" indicates the original transaction entry and "b" indicates the adjusting entry:

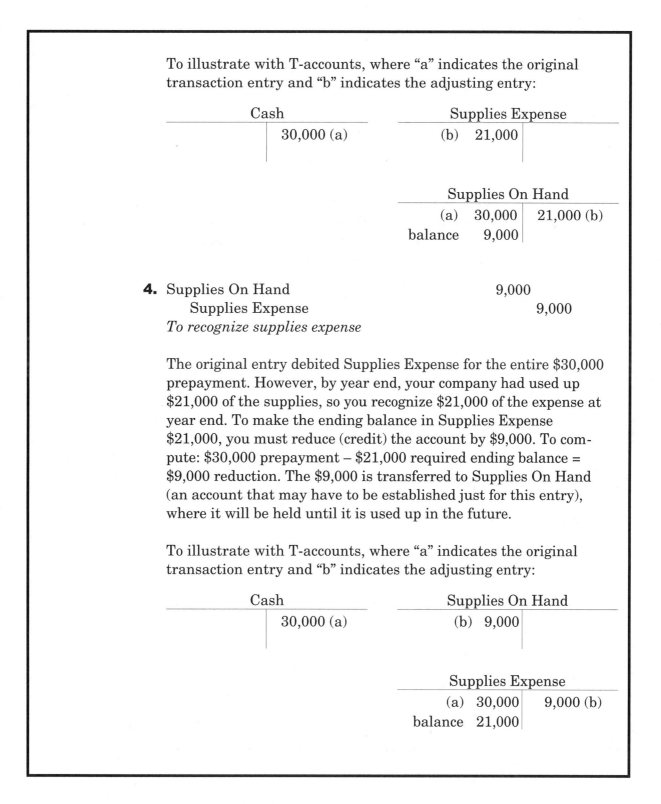

Cash	
30,000 (a)	

Supplies Expense	
(b) 21,000	

Supplies On Hand	
(a) 30,000	21,000 (b)
balance 9,000	

4. Supplies On Hand   9,000
       Supplies Expense   9,000
To recognize supplies expense

The original entry debited Supplies Expense for the entire $30,000 prepayment. However, by year end, your company had used up $21,000 of the supplies, so you recognize $21,000 of the expense at year end. To make the ending balance in Supplies Expense $21,000, you must reduce (credit) the account by $9,000. To compute: $30,000 prepayment – $21,000 required ending balance = $9,000 reduction. The $9,000 is transferred to Supplies On Hand (an account that may have to be established just for this entry), where it will be held until it is used up in the future.

To illustrate with T-accounts, where "a" indicates the original transaction entry and "b" indicates the adjusting entry:

Cash	
30,000 (a)	

Supplies On Hand	
(b) 9,000	

Supplies Expense	
(a) 30,000	9,000 (b)
balance 21,000	

Problem II.

Painting Expense	10,000	
Painting Advance		10,000

To record painting expense ($100,000 x 10%)

The original entry debited Painting Advance (prepaid painting expense) for the entire $12,000 prepayment. At year end, $10,000 must be transferred to Painting Expense to recognize the 10% of the job completed ($100,000 job x 10% completed = $10,000 expense that can be recognized). The remainder stays in Painting Advance until it is used up in the future.

Problem III.

Insurance Expense	4,000	
Unexpired Insurance		4,000

To record insurance expense ($1,000/month x 4 months)

The original entry debited Unexpired Insurance (prepaid insurance) for the entire $24,000 prepayment. At year end, $4,000 of the insurance has been used and therefore must be transferred to Insurance Expense to recognize the expense. The remainder stays in Unexpired Insurance until used up in the future.

Problem IV.

1. asset (same as Prepaid Insurance)

2. asset (same as Prepaid Supplies)

3. before

4. incurred

5. reduce

Problem V.

1. a

If the unused portion of the rent prepayment is not transferred out of Rent Expense and into Prepaid Rent, an asset account, assets will be understated.

2. b

Failure to reduce Prepaid Rent by the amount of the rent expense used up for the period will result in the balance in Prepaid Rent, an asset, being overstated and therefore overstating assets on the balance sheet.

3. d

$42,000 is the expense ($50,000 prepayment – $8,000 remaining at year end) and $8,000 is the balance remaining in Supplies On Hand until the $8,000 is used up.

4. a

5. a

An adjusting entry affects the income statement because it always involves an expense account, and it also affects the balance sheet because it always involves a prepaid (asset) account.

QUIZ 2   PREPAID (DEFERRED) EXPENSES

Problem I.

For each of the following, record the adjusting entry:

1. Your company prepays $18,000 of rent for 1 year and debits Rent Expense. Your company's year ends 4 months later.

2. Your company prepays $18,000 of rent for 1 year and debits Prepaid Rent. Your company's year ends 4 months later.

3. Your company buys $40,000 of office supplies and debits Supplies Expense. At year end, there are $6,000 of supplies unused (on hand).

4. Your company buys $40,000 of office supplies and debits Supplies On Hand. At year end, there are $6,000 of unused supplies left.

Problem II.

On November 1, your company signs up with a law firm for an agreed-upon retainer of $15,000 a year, paying the first 3 months' fee in advance and debiting Prepaid Legal Fees. Record the adjusting entry on December 31.

Problem III.

You prepay $24,000 for 1 year of insurance premiums and debit Unexpired Insurance (prepaid insurance expense). Your company's year ends 9 months later. Record the adjusting entry.

Problem IV.

Fill in the blanks.

1. Unused Supplies is a(n) _____ account.

2. Prepaid Insurance is a(n) _____ account.

3. A prepaid expense is cash paid (before/after) the expense is incurred.

4. An expense is booked when it is _____.

5. When you prepay insurance, you debit a(n) _____ account or a(n) _____ account and credit_____ .

Problem V.

Multiple choice. Circle the correct answer.

1. You prepay rent and debit Rent Expense. If part of the period paid for has elapsed and you do not record the adjusting entry, net income will be . . .

    a. understated
    b. overstated
    c. unaffected

2. You prepay rent and debit Prepaid Rent. If part of the time covered has elapsed and you do not record the adjusting entry, net income will be . . .

    a. understated
    b. overstated
    c. unaffected

3. Your company buys office supplies, debiting Supplies Inventory for $28,000. At year end, you estimate that $5,000 in unused supplies remain. The adjusting entry will leave an ending balance in Supplies Inventory of _____ and an ending balance in Supplies Expense of _____ .

    a. $28,000 and zero
    b. zero and $28,000
    c. $5,000 and $23,000
    d $23,000 and $5,000

Problem VI.

Write the number of the adjusting entry in Column B that belongs to the transaction entry in Column A:

A	B
1. Rent Expense	1. Prepaid Rent
Cash	Rent Expense
2. Prepaid Rent	2. Rent Expense
Cash	Prepaid Rent

QUIZ 2   Solutions and Explanations

Problem I.

1. Prepaid Rent   12,000
        Rent Expense   12,000
   To recognize rent expense ($18,000 – $6,000)

The original entry debited Rent Expense for the entire $18,000 prepayment. Because your company had used up (incurred) only four months' rent expense by year end, the ending balance in Rent Expense must be $6,000 (4/12 x $18,000). To achieve this balance, you must reduce (credit) the balance in Rent Expense by $12,000. To compute: $18,000 prepayment – $6,000 required ending balance = $12,000 reduction. This $12,000 is transferred to Prepaid Rent (an account that may have to be established just for this entry), where it will be held for future use.

2. Rent Expense   6,000
        Prepaid Rent   6,000
   To recognize rent expense ($1,500/month x 4 months)

The original entry debited Prepaid Rent for the entire $18,000 prepayment. At year end, the $6,000 (4/12 x $18,000) in rent used up must be transferred to Rent Expense.

3. Supplies On Hand   6,000
        Supplies Expense   6,000
   To recognize supplies expense

The original entry debited Supplies Expense for the entire $40,000 prepayment. But your company had used up only $34,000 of the supplies by year end, so you can recognize only $34,000 of the expense at year end. To make the ending balance in Supplies Expense equal $34,000, you must reduce (credit) the balance in the account by $6,000. To compute: $40,000 prepayment – $34,000 required ending balance = $6,000 reduction. This $6,000 is transferred to Supplies On Hand (an account that may have to be established just for this entry), where it is held until used up in the future.

4. Supplies Expense   34,000
     Supplies On Hand   34,000
To record supplies expense ($40,000 – $6,000)

The original entry debited Supplies On Hand for the entire $40,000 prepayment. At year end, the $34,000 must be transferred to Supplies Expense. The remainder stays in Supplies On Hand until it is used up in the future.

Problem II.

Legal Expense   2,500
     Prepaid Legal Fees   2,500
To record advance on law firm retainer

Although 3 months' expense was paid in advance, the date of payment was November 1, so only 2 months' expense can be recognized for the year (November and December). To compute: $15,000 annual retainer/12 months = $1,250/month x 2 months = $2,500.

Problem III.

Insurance Expense   18,000
     Unexpired Insurance   18,000
To record insurance expense ($2,000/month x 9 months)

Because the entire prepayment was recorded to Unexpired Insurance (prepaid insurance expense), the $18,000 of insurance used by year end must be transferred to Insurance Expense. To compute: $24,000 prepayment/12 months = $2,000 per month x 9 months = $18,000 insurance expense incurred.

Problem IV.

1. asset

2. asset

3. before

4. incurred

5. asset, expense, Cash

Problem V.

1. a
Unless the balance in Rent Expense is reduced to the amount of rent used, this balance will be too high, making overall expenses on the income statement too high and understating net income.

2. b
Unless the amount of rent used is transferred to Rent Expense at year end, the balance in Rent Expense will be too low, making overall expenses too low and overstating net income.

3. c
To compute: $28,000 advance – $5,000 in supplies remaining at year end = $23,000 in supplies expense for the year. Thus, the ending balance in Supplies Inventory will be $5,000, and the ending balance in Supplies Expense will be $23,000.

Problem VI.

1. 1

2. 2

Section 6
OTHER END-OF-PERIOD ENTRIES

Introduction

There are other accrual and deferral adjusting entries to be made besides the types discussed in Sections 2–5. Some result from deferrals previously made, such as when buildings and equipment are purchased and then depreciated. Some result from the necessity to accrue expenses incurred, such as bad debt expense. And there are other end-of-period journal entries that are neither accruals nor deferrals but merely transaction entries, such as entries to record interest earned and credited to a bank account or to a money market fund but not yet recorded on the books.

Adjusting Entries for Depreciation Expense

Depreciation is a way of matching an asset's cost against the income it helps to produce over time. To depreciate an asset, you must first determine its *depreciable base*, which is simply its original cost less its *residual value* (the estimated value that the asset will have when it can no longer be used).

For example, assume that a machine costs $110,000, has a residual value of $10,000 and an estimated life of 5 years. Under the simplest method of depreciation, the straight-line method, the company may take $20,000 depreciation expense in each of the 5 years. To compute: $110,000 cost – $10,000 residual value = $100,000 ÷ 5 years = $20,000 per year. (For a discussion of depreciation, see *Mastering Depreciation*.)

Assets that can be depreciated are known as operational assets. To be depreciable, assets must meet the following conditions:

- The asset must be tangible property, such as a building, equipment or furniture (land is not depreciable); and

- The asset cannot be held for resale (such as inventory) or for investment purposes (such as common stock); and

- The asset must have a useful life of more than 1 year when acquired.

The journal entry to record depreciation at year end is:

Depreciation Expense
    Accumulated Depreciation
To record depreciation expense

This entry is usually made at the end of the year, but like other adjusting entries, it can be made at the end of any accounting period.

PROBLEM 1: At the beginning of 20X1, LiCo purchases equipment at a cost of $5,000. Residual value is estimated at $200, and its useful life is estimated at 4 years. If LiCo uses straight-line depreciation, what is its annual depreciation expense?

SOLUTION 1: LiCo's annual depreciation expense is computed as follows:

$5,000 cost − $200 = $4,800 depreciable base

$4,800 depreciable base/4 years = $1,200 depreciation expense per year

The adjusting journal entry at year end is recorded as follows:

Depreciation Expense   1,200
    Accumulated Depreciation—Equipment   1,200
To record depreciation expense

This journal entry is recorded at the end of each of the 4 years of its estimated life: 20X1, 20X2, 20X3, and 20X4. At the end of 20X4, the fourth year, the equipment is fully depreciated, and no more depreciation expense can be taken.

PROBLEM 2: At the beginning of 20X1, LiCo buys property for $300,000, including land at $140,000 (land cannot be depreciated) and a building at $160,000. The building has an estimated residual value of $10,000 and an estimated life of 30 years. If LiCo depreciates the building under the straight-line method, what is its annual depreciation expense?

SOLUTION 2: LiCo's annual depreciation expense is computed as follows:

$160,000 − $10,000 = $150,000 depreciable base

$150,000 depreciable base/30 years = $5,000 depreciation expense per year

The adjusting journal entry at year end is recorded as follows:

Depreciation Expense   5,000
    Accumulated Depreciation—Building   5,000
To record depreciation expense

LiCo records this journal entry at the end of each year for 30 years.

In practice, however, LiCo would use a single adjusting journal entry for all its depreciable assets. The single adjusting journal entry at year end is recorded as follows:

Depreciation Expense   6,200
    Accumulated Depreciation—Equipment   1,200
    Accumulated Depreciation—Building   5,000
To record depreciation expense

Depreciation expense is an expense on the income statement. Total assets and total accumulated depreciation amounts appear on the balance sheet. The accumulated depreciation account (that is, the total expense taken over the years) reduces the book value of the asset. Combining the data from Problems 1 and 2, these accounts will appear on LiCo's 20X1 balance sheet as follows:

Property, plant and equipment (PP&E)
    Land—at cost   140,000
    Buildings—at cost   160,000
    Less: Accumulated Depreciation   5,000   155,000

    Equipment—at cost   5,000
    Less: Accumulated depreciation   1,200   3,800
    Total PP&E   298,800

Each year, the balance in LiCo's accumulated depreciation account will increase as another year of depreciation expense is added for each depreciable asset. The book value of LiCo's total PP&E will decrease.

In reality, depreciation expense for all depreciable assets is computed, then recorded on the depreciation schedule. The year-end adjustment is then copied onto the trial balance, and the adjusting entry is recorded in the general journal.

Adjusting Entries
for Bad Debt Expense

Bad debt *expense* is an estimate of the portion of credit sales (or accounts receivable) that the company does not expect to collect. The adjusting entry to record the estimate of bad debt expense is as follows:

> Bad Debt Expense
>   Allowance For Doubtful Accounts
> *To record bad debt expense*

Of course, the year-end entry is only an estimate. The year-end balance in Allowance For Doubtful Accounts becomes the next year's beginning balance (Bad Debt Expense is closed out at year end with all the other revenue and expense accounts).

For instance, assume that at the end of 20X0, your company's first year in business, you record the following adjusting entry for bad debt expense:

> December 31, 20X0
>
> | | | |
> |---|---|---|
> | Bad Debt Expense | 5,000 | |
> | Allowance For Doubtful Accounts | | 5,000 |
> | *To record bad debt expense* | | |

Your company's 20X0 ending balance in Allowance For Doubtful Accounts is $5,000, and its 20X1 *beginning* balance in Allowance For Doubtful Accounts is the same $5,000.

The key word is "doubtful." This is the amount your company *thinks* it will never collect. During 20X1, as it is determined that particular customers will not be paying their bills, you move the appropriate amounts from the doubtful category to the "sure" category.

For instance, assume that on March 3, 20X1, BadCo goes out of business, and you determine that your company will not collect $1,250 due from BadCo. You must move the $1,250 from the "doubtful" category to the "absolutely uncollectible" category, as follows:

Allowance For Doubtful Accounts	1,250	(It is no longer doubtful; it is definitely not being paid.)
Accounts Receivable	1,250	(Remove this uncollectible from accounts receivable.)
To write off uncollectible accounts		

To illustrate, assume that your company's Allowance For Doubtful Accounts during the first half of 20X1 appears as follows:

Allowance For Doubtful Accounts			
		5,000	Balance 1/1/20X1
3/3	1,250		
3/27	3,000		
4/12	125		
5/31	350		
		275	Balance 5/31/20X1

When management underestimates bad debt. As 20X1 continues, your company's estimate of bad debts turns out to have been too low. As you learn of new uncollectible accounts, you continue to credit Accounts Receivable and debit Allowance For Doubtful Accounts *even if you go beyond the beginning balance of $5,000*, as follows (amounts are assumed):

Allowance For Doubtful Accounts			
		5,000	Balance 1/1/20X1
3/3	1,250		
3/27	3,000		
4/12	125		
5/31	350		
6/10	1,000		
8/31	200		
Balance 5/31/20X1	925		

By year end, Allowance For Doubtful Accounts has a debit balance instead of a credit balance. A new year-end adjusting entry will reestablish a credit balance in the account.

Recording Bad Debt Expense for Tax Purposes v. Book Purposes

***For tax purposes:* The direct write-off method.** Under the direct write-off method, which is required by the IRS for income tax purposes, bad debt expense is taken when the company determines that a particular receivable cannot be collected. (This method *cannot* be used for book purposes under generally accepted accounting principles.) Very small companies sometimes use this method for both tax and book purposes.

***For book purposes:* The allowance method.** Under this method, which is required by GAAP, there are two ways to account for bad debts:

1. Estimate bad debt as a percentage of credit sales. Under this method, at year end, management estimates the percentage of credit sales that it may not collect. This estimate is recorded as follows:

> Bad Debt Expense
> > Allowance For Doubtful Accounts

> **EXAMPLE 1: Bad debt as a percentage of credit sales.** For 20X5, SimCo has credit sales of $200,000. Based on past experience, the company estimates that bad debt loss for the year will be 2% of credit sales. SimCo records its bad debt loss for book purposes (as opposed to tax purposes) for the year as follows:

> | | | |
> |---|---|---|
> | Bad Debt Expense | 4,000 | |
> | Allowance For Doubtful Accounts | | 4,000 |
> | *To record bad debt expense* | | |

> At the end of each year (or other period), SimCo will record its estimate of bad debt with a debit to Bad Debt Expense and a credit to Allowance For Doubtful Accounts.

2. Estimate the percentage of accounts receivable that will not be collected. This estimate is based on aging receivables (the older accounts receivable are, the more likely they are to be uncollectible). Whatever the dollar amount of the estimate, it must become the ending balance in the Allowance For Doubtful Accounts. Thus, recording bad debt expense under the percentage of accounts receivable method requires the following steps:

> 1. Find out from management what dollar amount of total receivables it does not expect to collect. *This amount must become the ending balance in the Allowance For Doubtful Accounts.*

> 2. Check the current balance in the Allowance For Doubtful Accounts to see how much it must be either increased or decreased to arrive at the required ending balance. The journal entry that you record for bad debt expense must give you the required ending balance in the Allowance For Doubtful Accounts.

EXAMPLE 2: When there is a credit balance in Allowance For Doubtful Accounts. At year-end 20X6, DruCo has accounts receivable of $90,000 and estimates that bad debt will be 5% of these accounts receivable. Thus, bad debt for the year is estimated at $4,500 ($90,000 x 5%). DruCo's Allowance For Doubtful Accounts has a current credit balance of $3,000. Therefore, DruCo must increase the balance by $1,500 to arrive at the required ending balance of $4,500 ($3,000 current balance + $1,500 increase = $4,500 ending credit balance) as follows:

Bad Debt Expense	1,500	
Allowance For Doubtful Accounts		1,500

To record bad debt expense

This is a fairly typical year-end adjustment. But, as explained earlier, when more accounts receivable are written off during the year than management estimated, the Allowance For Doubtful Accounts may end up with a debit balance.

EXAMPLE 3: When there is a debit balance in Allowance For Doubtful Accounts. During 20X7, DruCo discovers that it significantly underestimated its bad debt. By year end, the Allowance For Doubtful Accounts has a *debit* balance of $2,000. At year-end 20X7, DruCo has accounts receivable of $45,000 and estimates that bad debt will be 10% of accounts receivable, or $4,500 ($45,000 x 10%).

Because the Allowance For Doubtful Accounts currently has a *debit* balance of $2,000, DruCo must add this $2,000 to the desired ending credit balance of $4,500 to determine the amount of the credit to the Allowance For Doubtful Accounts ($4,500 desired ending credit balance + $2,000 debit balance = $6,500 credit to the account), as follows:

Bad Debt Expense	6,500	
Allowance For Doubtful Accounts		6,500

To record bad debt expense

This entry can be illustrated with a T-account (amounts are assumed):

Allowance For Doubtful Accounts

12/31/X7 before AJE 2,000*	
	6,500 AJE on 12/31/X7

(To produce the correct ending balance of $4,5(in the account require(credit of $6,500.)

*$3,000 opening credit balance – $5,000 debit balance from accounts actually written off during the year = $2,000 debit balance on 12/31/X7 before the AJE is made.

How Bad Debt Appears on the Financial Statements

Bad debt is an expense on the income statement. The allowance for doubtful accounts appears on the balance sheet with total accounts receivable. The difference between accounts receivable and doubtful accounts (Accounts Receivable – Allowance For Doubtful Accounts) is the *net realizable value*. This is the amount that the company expects ultimately to collect from customers. Just as accumulated depreciation reduces the book value of the asset, allowance for doubtful accounts reduces the book value of accounts receivable.

Year-End Entries for Certain Cash Accounts

Some cash accounts may earn interest, such as interest-earning bank accounts, money market accounts, stock brokerage accounts, or other accounts. It may be necessary to record interest credited to your account by the bank but not yet recorded in your company's books as follows:

      Cash—Savings
         Interest Revenue

or

      Cash—Money Market
         Interest Revenue

These entries increase assets on the balance sheet and also increase revenues on the income statement.

Such entries are normal transaction entries, rather than *adjusting* entries, because they do not result from either accruals or deferrals. (Remember, an *adjusting* entry does not involve the Cash account.)

QUIZ 1   OTHER END-OF-PERIOD ENTRIES

Problem I.

Multiple choice. Circle the correct answer.

1. Which of the following accounts is not depreciated?

    a. Equipment
    b. Furniture
    c. Land
    d. Building

2. A piece of equipment costs $20,000. The estimated residual value is $2,000, and it is estimated to have a 4-year life. If the company uses straight-line depreciation, then depreciation expense for Years 1 and 2, respectively, will be . . .

    a. $4,500 and $4,500
    b. $5,000 and $5,000
    c. $4,500 and $5,000
    d. $5,000 and $4,500

3. A company has credit sales for the year of $100,000. Bad debt is estimated at 3% of credit sales. The allowance for doubtful accounts has a credit balance of $1,000. The adjusting entry at year end will include a debit to bad debt expense of . . .

    a. zero   b. $1,000   c. $2,000   d. $3,000

4. A company has ending accounts receivable of $100,000. Its desired allowance for doubtful accounts is estimated at 4% of accounts receivable. Allowance For Doubtful Accounts currently has a credit balance of $1,000. The adjusting entry at year end will include . . .

    a. a debit to Allowance For Doubtful Accounts of $1,000
    b. a credit to Allowance For Doubtful Accounts of $3,000
    c. a debit to Allowance For Doubtful Accounts of $5,000
    d. a credit to Allowance For Doubtful Accounts of $5,000

5. A company has ending accounts receivable of $100,000, of which it estimates that 4% will not be collectible. Allowance For Doubtful Accounts currently has a debit balance of $1,000. The adjusting entry at year end will include . . .

    a. a debit to Allowance For Doubtful Accounts of $1,000
    b. a credit to Allowance For Doubtful Accounts of $3,000
    c. a debit to Allowance For Doubtful Accounts of $5,000
    d. a credit to Allowance For Doubtful Accounts of $5,000

Problem II.

Mark each statement True or False.

1. The adjusting entry to record depreciation expense debits Accumulated Depreciation.

    a. True   b. False

2. To record bad debts for book purposes under either the percentage of credit sales or the percentage of accounts receivable method, debit Bad Debt Expense and credit Allowance For Doubtful Accounts for the amount of the estimated bad debt expense for the year.

    a. True   b. False

3. Recording bad debt expense under the direct write-off method is acceptable for tax purposes but cannot be used for book purposes under generally accepted accounting principles.

    a. True   b. False

4. Allowance For Doubtful Accounts always has a credit balance.

    a. True   b. False

QUIZ 1   Solutions and Explanations

Problem I.

1. c

2. a

$20,000 cost – $2,000 residual value = $18,000 depreciable base ÷ 4 years = $4,500 per year depreciation expense over each of the 4 years of its life.

3. d

3% x $100,000 = $3,000 bad debt expense for the year. When bad debt is based on a percentage of credit sales, the adjusting entry is for the estimated amount regardless of the balance in Allowance For Doubtful Accounts.

4. b

4% x $100,000 = $4,000 allowance for doubtful accounts at year end. Under the accounts receivable method for estimating bad debt, the ending balance in the Allowance For Doubtful Accounts must be $4,000. To compute: $1,000 credit balance in the Allowance For Doubtful Accounts + $3,000 credit = $4,000 desired balance.

5. d

4% x $100,000 = $4,000 desired balance in Allowance For Doubtful Accounts. Under the accounts receivable method for estimating bad debts, the ending balance in the Allowance For Doubtful Accounts must be $4,000. Currently, the account has a *debit* balance of $1,000, so a $5,000 credit must be added to yield the correct credit balance of $4,000. To compute: $4,000 estimate of bad debt expense (required ending balance) + $1,000 debit balance = $5,000 increase required. Thus, the Allowance For Doubtful Accounts must be credited for $5,000.

To illustrate with a T-account:

Allowance For Doubtful Accounts

current balance 1,000	
	5,000 AJE
	4,000 Ending Balance

(Management estimated that bad debt would be $4,000 for the year. To achieve this ending balance, the account must be credited for $5,000.)

Problem II.

1. False

The adjusting entry to record depreciation expense debits the expense account, Depreciation Expense, and credits the balance sheet account, Accumulated Depreciation.

2. False

Only under the percentage of credit sales method do you credit Allowance For Doubtful Accounts by the amount of bad debt expense. Under the percentage of accounts receivable method, the ending credit balance in Allowance For Doubtful Accounts must *equal* management's estimate of uncollectible accounts, so the adjusting entry must result in the correct ending balance.

3. True

4. False

Every time a company writes off an accounts receivable that becomes uncollectible, it debits Allowance For Doubtful Accounts (and credits Accounts Receivable). If more accounts are written off than the company anticipated, constantly debiting Allowance For Doubtful Accounts will eventually result in a debit balance.

QUIZ 2   OTHER END-OF-PERIOD ENTRIES

Problem I.

Multiple choice. Circle the correct answer.

1. Net realizable value of accounts receivable is . . .

    a. the total of all accounts receivable

    b. the total of all accounts receivable plus the allowance for doubtful accounts

    c. the total of all of accounts receivable less the allowance for doubtful accounts

    d. the total of all accounts receivable plus bad debt expense

2. A building is acquired at a cost of $400,000. It is estimated to have a 40-year life and a residual value of $40,000. If the building is depreciated under the straight-line method, annual depreciation expense will be . . .

    a. $400,000   b. $40,000   c. $10,000   d. $9,000

3. A company has credit sales of $300,000 for the year and bad debt is estimated at 2% of credit sales. Allowance for Doubtful Accounts has a credit balance of $2,000. The adjusting entry for bad debt will debit Bad Debt Expense for . . .

    a. $6,000   b. $4,000   c. $2,000   d. zero

4. A company estimates bad debt at 2% of ending accounts receivable, which has an ending balance of $250,000. If Allowance For Doubtful Accounts has a credit balance of $3,000, the adjusting entry to record bad debt will debit Bad Debt Expense for . . .

    a. $5,000   b. $3,000   c. $2,000   d. zero

5. A company estimates bad debt at 2% of ending accounts receivable, which has an ending balance of $250,000. If Allowance For Doubtful Accounts has a debit balance of $3,000, the adjusting entry for bad debt is a debit to Bad Debt Expense for . . .

    a. $8,000   b. $5,000   c. $2,000   d. zero

Problem II.

Mark each statement True or False.

1. The journal entry to record depreciation expense credits Accumulated Depreciation.

    a. True   b. False

2. A debit balance in Allowance For Doubtful Accounts means that in prior years, bad debt expense was underestimated.

    a. True   b. False

3. The entry to record bad debt expense for book purposes debits Bad Debt Expense.

    a. True   b. False

4. Net realizable value is an income statement account.

    a. True   b. False

5. The entry to record interest revenue for a money market account debits an asset account.

    a. True   b. False

6. Net realizable value is Accounts Receivable less Allowance For Doubtful Accounts.

    a. True   b. False

7. To write off an accounts receivable under the allowance method, credit Allowance For Doubtful Accounts.

    a. True   b. False

QUIZ 2   *Solutions and Explanations*

Problem I.

1. c

2. d

$400,000 cost – $40,000 residual value = $360,000 depreciable base ÷ 40 years = $9,000 depreciation expense per year

3. a

$300,000 x 2% = $6,000. When bad debt expense is computed as a percentage of credit sales, the amount used in the adjusting entry is found simply by multiplying total credit sales by the percentage of estimated bad debt. The balance in Allowance For Doubtful Accounts before the adjusting entry is recorded is irrelevant.

4. c

$250,000 x 2% = $5,000 – $3,000 current balance = $2,000 increase required in the Allowance For Doubtful Accounts credit balance.

5. a

$250,000 x 2% = $5,000 final credit balance needed in Allowance For Doubtful Accounts + $3,000 current debit balance = $8,000 increase (credit) required in the adjusting entry.

To illustrate in a T-account:

Allowance For Doubtful Accounts	
Current Balance 3,000	
	8,000 AJE
	5,000 Ending Balance

Problem II.

1. True

Every year when Depreciation Expense is debited for that year's expenses, Accumulated Depreciation is credited, increasing the balance in this account. This continues until the asset has been fully depreciated.

2. True

At the end of each year Allowance For Doubtful Accounts is credited, leaving a credit balance in the account. During the year, whenever management determines that an account is uncollectible (has moved from the "doubtful" to "uncollectible"), Allowance For Doubtful Accounts is debited and Accounts Receivable is credited. Thus, when more accounts are written off than management estimated, the debits to Allowance For Doubtful Accounts will result in a debit balance.

3. True

The credit is to Allowance For Doubtful Accounts.

4. False

Net realizable value is not an account. It is a line on the balance sheet that shows the accounts receivable that the company expects to collect.

5. True

The credit is to Interest Revenue.

6. True

7. False

Debit Allowance For Doubtful Accounts and credit Accounts Receivable.

Section 7
FROM UNADJUSTED TRIAL BALANCE TO FINANCIAL STATEMENTS

The Chart of Accounts

All organizations, from "mom and pop" sole proprietorships to large corporations such as General Motors, follow a similar pattern in their chart of accounts, as follows:

If the account is a(n)...	Then it will usually have a number from...
Asset account	100 to 199
Liability account	200 to 299
Owners' Equity account	300 to 399
Income account	400 to 499
Expense account	500 to 599

Within each category, each account has its own number. For example:

ASSETS

103	Cash
108	Bank
112	Inventories
132	Furniture and Fixtures
147	Automobiles
Etc.	

LIABILITIES

206	Accounts Payable—General
207	Accounts Payable—Parts Suppliers
209	Accounts Payable—Packaging Suppliers
Etc.	

There are many variations because each business has its own numbering system. For example, instead of 100, 200, etc., the accounts may be numbered 1,000, 2,000, etc.:

ASSETS

1004   Cash
1010   Bank
1202   Inventories
1444   Furniture and Fixtures
1587   Automobiles
Etc.

LIABILITIES

2214   Accounts Payable—General
2225   Accounts Payable—Parts Suppliers
2906   Accounts Payable—Packaging Suppliers
Etc.

Or, if a company has many assets, it may use the 100 or 1,000 category for current assets and the 200 or 2,000 category for Equipment and further categorize accounts with a letter after the last digit:

ASSETS

101A   Petty Cash Fund
101B   Stamp Fund—Mail Room
102A   Cash in Bank
103   Accounts Receivable Control
103F   Frames
103P   Parts
103T   Turbine parts
Etc.

LIABILITIES

201   Accounts Payable
202   Notes Payable
208   Bonds Payable
Etc.

Or, a small firm may use a simple list from 1 to 100 to cover all accounts from assets and liabilities to income and expenses.

The following example illustrates a typical company's chart of accounts by showing the categories and kinds of accounts. A real company, however, would probably have many more accounts, such as numerous expense items.

EXAMPLE OF A TYPICAL CHART OF ACCOUNTS

Account Number	Account
100	Cash—Checking
101	Cash—Savings
102	Accounts Receivable
103	Allowance For Doubtful Accounts
104	Inventory
105	Prepaid Insurance
110	Land
111	Plant And Equipment
112	Accumulated Depreciation
200	Accounts Payable
201	Expenses Payable
202	Income Taxes Payable
210	Notes Payable - Short Term
220	Notes Payable - Long Term
230	Mortgage Payable
300	Common Stock
301	Paid-In Capital In Excess of Par
310	Retained Earnings
400	Sales
410	Interest Revenue
500	Purchases
505	Cost of Sales
510	Advertising Expense
511	Bad Debt Expense
512	Depreciation Expense
514	Insurance Expense
516	Interest Expense
517	Legal and Accounting Expense
518	Repairs and Maintenance Expense
519	Salaries Expense
520	Utility Expense
600	Gains
700	Losses

Accounts numbered 300–399 are owners' equity accounts. If the entity shown above were a sole proprietorship, the 300 account would not be Common Stock, but instead would be Jones [or other individual's name], Capital. If the entity were a partnership, the 300 account would be a particular partner's capital account and there would be a similar account for each partner.

The *order* of accounts in all charts of accounts is the same:

Asset accounts
Liability accounts
Owners' equity accounts
Income accounts
Expense accounts

From Company Chart of Accounts to Company Financial Statements

To begin the process of preparing financial statements, prepare the unadjusted trial balance by listing all the accounts in the general ledger on a worksheet. A computerized accounting program will automatically list the accounts on a worksheet. Then follow these steps:

1. Prepare the unadjusted trial balance from the general ledger accounts.

2. Enter the adjustments (these are the adjusting entries learned earlier).

3. Combine the unadjusted trial balance with the adjustments to prepare the adjusted trial balance.

4. Extend the amounts from the adjusted trial balance to the appropriate financial statement columns.

Step 1. Prepare the unadjusted trial balance. Below is a simplified worksheet for a sole proprietorship:

Jones Company Worksheet
December 31, 20X7

	Unadjusted Trial Balance		Adjustments		Adjusted Trial Balance		Income Statement		Balance Sheet	
	Dr	Cr	Dr	Cr	Dr	Cr	Dr	Cr	Dr	Cr
Cash	800									
Accounts Receivable	1,000									
Prepaid Rent	200									
Wages Payable		500								
Capital, Jones		600								
Withdrawals	200									
Revenue		2,000								
Wages Expense	400									
Rent Expense	500									
Total	3,100	3,100								
Net Income										

- The accounts are listed in the order of a standard chart of accounts: assets, liabilities, owners' equity, revenues, and expenses.

- If an account has a debit balance, the balance is presented in the column marked "Dr" (the abbreviation for debit). If an account has a credit balance, the balance is presented in the column marked "Cr" (the abbreviation for credit). When all the account balances are added up, the total of all debit balances should equal the total of all credit balances. On the Jones Company worksheet, the two sums are equal, so the trial balance is said to be "in balance."

The Computerized
Unadjusted Trial Balance

Most computer software packages automatically generate a trial balance. Many do not separate total debits from total credits, but instead show only one column of account balances, marking debits with a "+," credits with a "–," and showing the sum at the bottom. For example:

Cash	+100
Receivables	+300
Payables	– 50
Capital	–150
Revenues	–400
Expenses	+200
TOTAL	0

Because the sum is zero, this trial balance is in balance.

When Total Debits Do Not
Equal Total Credits

When total debits do not equal total credits (or on the computer, when the sum is not zero), you must locate and correct the error(s) before proceeding. Sometimes total debits and credits are equal, but there are still errors. For example, if your company paid rent of $150, but mistakenly debited Rent Expense for only $100 and credited Cash for only $100, total debits would still equal total credits, despite the $50 error in the Rent Expense and Cash accounts. Techniques for locating and correcting errors on the trial balance are explained in *Mastering Correction of Accounting Errors I*.

A common cause of errors on a trial balance is that a debit balance is listed in the credit balance column, or a credit balance is listed in the debit balance column. Figure 7-1 (page 97) presents a guide for making sure that each account balance in any trial balance, unadjusted or adjusted, has been listed in the proper column.

FIGURE 7-1
Normal Balances of Various Ledger Accounts

Account	Normal Balance	
Balance sheet accounts		
Asset accounts		
Cash	Debit balance	
[Various titles] Receivable	Debit balance	
Allowance for Doubtful Accounts		Credit balance
Inventory	Debit balance	
Prepaid [Various titles]	Debit balance	
Land	Debit balance	
Building	Debit balance	
Equipment	Debit balance	
Accumulated Depreciation—[Various titles]		Credit balance
Liability accounts		
[Various titles] Payable		Credit balance
Discount on Bonds Payable	Debit balance	
[Various titles] Revenue in Advance		Credit balance
or Unearned [Various titles] Revenue		Credit balance
Owners' equity accounts		
Capital [Common and/or Preferred] Stock*		Credit balance
Retained Earnings*		Credit balance
Treasury Stock	Debit balance	
Income statement accounts		
Revenue accounts		
[Various titles] Revenue		Credit balance
Sales Returns and Allowances	Debit balance	
Expense accounts		
Purchases	Debit balance	
Freight-In	Debit balance	
Purchase Discounts		Credit balance
Purchase Returns and Allowances		Credit balance
Cost of Goods Sold	Debit balance	
[Various titles] Expense	Debit balance	
[Various titles] Loss	Debit balance	
[Various titles] Gain		Credit balance
Statement of retained earnings accounts		
Dividends Declared**	Debit balance	

*If the entity is a partnership or sole proprietorship, the account Owner's Capital (normal credit balance) is used and it appears on the statement of capital.

**If the entity is a partnership or sole proprietorship, the account Withdrawal is used; this account appears on the statement of capital.

Step 2. Enter the adjustments. Adjusting entries are required for entities that use *accrual basis* accounting because revenue is recognized only when earned, not when collected, and expenses are recognized only when incurred, not when paid. (If a company uses a true form of *cash basis* accounting, it recognizes revenue when cash is received and recognizes expenses when cash is paid and makes no adjusting entries. However, most companies claiming to operate on a cash basis actually operate on a *modified cash basis* under which they make adjustments for depreciation, but do not make other adjustments.)

When accrual basis companies prepare financial statements, they must decide what period of time the statements cover: a year, a quarter, a month or other period. Every financial statement has a cut-off date: the last day of the period that the statement covers. On that date the company cuts off the revenue earned and expenses incurred that will appear on the financial statements. The adjusting entries bring expense and revenue accounts up to date as of the cut-off date.

To summarize the two types of adjusting entries:

1. *Accruals.* These adjusting entries record revenue earned but not yet collected (for example, your company earned interest revenue, but had not received payment by the cut-off date), or expenses incurred but not paid (your company owed employee salaries, but had not paid them by the cut-off date).

2. *Prepayments (deferrals).* These adjusting entries are required because previous transaction entries were made to record payments of expenses before the expenses were incurred or to record receipt of revenue before the revenue had been earned. The adjusting entries adjust expense accounts to reflect the proper amount of expense incurred by the cut-off date and adjust revenue accounts to reflect the proper amount of revenue earned by the cut-off date.

The Jones Company's adjustments on December 31, 19X7 appear on the worksheet (on page 99) in the Adjustments column. Each adjustment is given a letter so that anyone reading the worksheet can see which debits are related to which credits. For example, in adjusting entry "a," Accounts Receivable was debited and Revenue was credited. In adjusting entry "b," Wages Expense was debited and Wages Payable was credited.

Jones Company Worksheet
December 31, 20X7

	Unadjusted Trial Balance		Adjustments		Adjusted Trial Balance		Income Statement		Balance Sheet	
	Dr	Cr	Dr	Cr	Dr	Cr	Dr	Cr	Dr	Cr
Cash	800									
Accounts Receivable	1,000		(a) 100							
Prepaid Rent	200			(c) 40						
Wages Payable		500		(b) 150						
Capital, Jones		600								
Withdrawals	200									
Revenue		2,000		(a) 100						
Wages Expense	400		(b) 150							
Rent Expense	500		(c) 40							
Total	3,100	3,100	290	290						
Net Income										

In the adjustments column, total debits equal total credits, so Jones Company now records these adjustments as adjusting journal entries in the general journal, as follows:

a.	Accounts Receivable	100	
	Revenue		100
	To record revenue		
b.	Wages Expense	150	
	Wages Payable		150
	To accrue wages expense		
c.	Rent Expense	40	
	Prepaid rent		40
	To recognize rent expense		

Each letter next to the journal entry in the general journal corresponds to the letter of the adjustment on the worksheet. After these entries are recorded in the general journal, they are posted to each account shown in the general ledger.

The Jones Company is now ready to combine Columns 1 and 2 with Columns 3 and 4 to prepare the adjusted trial balance.

Step 3. Prepare the adjusted trial balance. Jones Company now completes the adjusted trial balance, as follows:

Each debit and credit balance from the unadjusted trial balance is extended to the adjusted trial balance. For example, the Capital, Jones $600 credit balance in the "unadjusted" column is extended to the "adjusted" column. The adjusted trial balance is presented as follows:

Jones Company Worksheet
December 31, 20X7

	Unadjusted Trial Balance		Adjustments		Adjusted Trial Balance		Income Statement		Balance Sheet	
	Dr	**Cr**	**Dr**	**Cr**	**Dr**	**Cr**	**Dr**	**Cr**	**Dr**	**Cr**
Cash	800				800					
Accounts Receivable	1,000		(a) 100		1,100					
Prepaid Rent	200			(c) 40	160					
Wages Payable		500		(b) 150		650				
Capital, Jones		600				600				
Withdrawals	200				200					
Revenue		2,000		(a) 100		2,100				
Wages Expense	400		(b) 150		550					
Rent Expense	500		(c) 40		540					
Total	3,100	3,100	290	290	3,350	3,350				
Net Income										

In the lines with adjustments, the balance in the unadjusted trial balance is combined with the adjustment to yield a new balance in the adjusted trial balance column.

The following shows the arithmetic involved in extending each line across the worksheet:

	Unadjusted Trial Balance		Adjustments		Adjusted Trial Balance	
	Dr	**Cr**	**Dr**	**Cr**	**Dr**	**Cr**
Accounts Receivable	1,000		+100		=1,100	
Prepaid Rent	200			− 40	= 160	
Wages Payable		500		+150		= 650

Or, to put it in words:

- $1,000 Accounts Receivable debit balance (unadjusted) + $100 debit (adjustment) = $1,100 Accounts Receivable debit balance (adjusted).

- $200 Prepaid Rent debit balance (unadjusted) − $40 credit (adjustment) = $160 Prepaid Rent debit balance (adjusted).

- $500 Wages Payable credit balance (unadjusted) + $150 credit (adjustment) = $650 Wages Payable credit balance (adjusted).

And so on.

In the Adjustments column, total debits equal total credits, so there is no need to look for errors.

Step 4. Prepare the income statement. Although this course goes only through the adjusted trial balance, the remaining steps show how the adjusted trial balance fits in the accounting process.

To prepare the income statement, the revenue and expense balances are extended to the income statement debit and credit columns. To determine the company's net income or net loss, total the income statement's debits column and credits column. If total credits are greater than total debits, the company made a profit, so there is net income. If total debits are greater than total credits, the company has a net loss.

Jones Company Worksheet
December 31, 20X7

	Unadjusted Trial Balance		Adjustments		Adjusted Trial Balance		Income Statement		Balance Sheet	
	Dr	Cr	Dr	Cr	Dr	Cr	Dr	Cr	Dr	Cr
Cash	800				800					
Accounts Receivable	1,000		(a) 100		1,100					
Prepaid Rent	200			(c) 40	160					
Wages Payable		500		(b) 150		650				
Capital, Jones		600				600				
Withdrawals	200				200					
Revenue		2,000		(a) 100		2,100		2,100		
Wages Expense	400		(b) 150		550		550			
Rent Expense	500		(c) 40		540		540			
Total	3,100	3,100	290	290	3,350	3,350	1,090	2,100		
Net Income							1,010*			
							2,100	2,100		

*$2,100 total revenues − $1,090 total expenses = $1,010 net income before taxes.

To assure that total debits equal total credits, net income is entered in the debit column (if there had been a net loss, the net loss would have been entered in the credit column.)

Step 5. Prepare the balance sheet. To prepare the balance sheet, extend the assets, liabilities and owners' equity account balances to the appropriate balance sheet debit and credit columns. *Exception:* Net income is extended from the *debits* column of the income statement to the *credits* column of the balance sheet, because it is added to the Capital account (sole proprietorship or partnership) or to the Retained Earnings account (corporation). These accounts have a credit balance.

Jones Company Worksheet
December 31, 20X7

	Unadjusted Trial Balance		Adjustments		Adjusted Trial Balance		Income Statement		Balance Sheet	
	Dr	Cr	Dr	Cr	Dr	Cr	Dr	Cr	Dr	Cr
Cash	800				800				800	
Accounts Receivable	1,000		(a) 100		1,100				1,100	
Prepaid Rent	200			(c) 40	160				160	
Wages Payable		500		(b) 150		650				650
Capital, Jones		600				600				600
Withdrawals	200				200				200	
Revenue		2,000		(a) 100		2,100		2,100		
Wages Expense	400		(b) 150		550		550			
Rent Expense	500		(c) 40		540		540			
Total	3,100	3,100	290	290	3,350	3,350	1,090	2,100	2,260	1,250
Net Income							1,010*			1,010*
							2,100	2,100	2,260	2,260

*Net income was extended from the income statement *debits* column (where it was put to assure that total debits and credits equal) to the balance sheet *credits* column because it is added to the Capital account, which has a credit balance. Now in the balance sheet column, total debits equal total credits.

With the worksheet complete, the financial statements may be prepared and distributed to the appropriate parties.

Preparing the Financial Statements from the Worksheet

To prepare the financial statements, use the amounts from the worksheet income statement and balance sheet columns. Below are the three financial statements for a sole proprietorship in their proper format.

1. The income statement, also called the "earnings statement" or "profit and loss statement," is dated for the period it covers. For Jones Company, the income statement covers one year. A statement covering a shorter period might say "For the *month* ended . . .," "For the *quarter* ended . . .," "For *the six months* ended . . ." or for another period.

Jones Company
Income Statement
For the year ended December 31, 20X7

Revenue		$2,100
Less:		
Wages expense	$ 550	
Rent expense	540	
Total expenses		1,090
Net income		$1,010

2. The balance sheet. Jones Company is a sole proprietorship, so the owners' equity account is "Capital." If Jones were a corporation, the owners' equity accounts would include Capital Stock and Retained Earnings.

Jones Company
Balance Sheet
As of December 31, 20X7

Assets

Cash	$ 800
Receivables	1,100
Prepaid rent	160
Total assets	$2,060

Liabilities and Capital

Payables	$ 650
Capital	1,410
Total liabilities and Capital	$2,060

3. **The statement of capital.** Below is the statement of capital, which is used by sole proprietorships. If Jones Company were a corporation, this would be the statement of retained earnings.

Jones Company
Statement of Capital
For the year ended December 31, 20X7

Beginning capital	$ 600
Add:	
Net income	1,010
	1,610
Less:	
Withdrawals	200
Ending capital	$1,410

Closing Entries

After the financial statements have been prepared, the books are closed, a process in which the balances in the revenue, expense and withdrawal accounts are reduced to zero so that in the next year these accounts will start with nothing in them.

The Post-closing Trial Balance

After the books are closed, a *post-closing* trial balance is taken *from the general ledger account balances*. This trial balance is compared to the worksheet to make sure that adjustments were recorded from the worksheet to the general ledger. This trial balance includes only balance sheet accounts (because the revenue and expense accounts were closed out), and the preparer makes sure that total debits equal total credits.

QUIZ 1 FROM UNADJUSTED TRIAL BALANCE TO FINANCIAL STATEMENTS

Problem I.

Fill in the blanks.

1. In an unadjusted trial balance, the accounts are listed in the same order as in the chart of accounts, which is _____ followed by _____, _____, _____ and _____.

2. Adjusting entries make expense and revenue accounts current as of the _____ date.

3. Accruals record revenue _____, but not _____, or expenses _____, but not _____.

4. Deferrals record _____ of revenue not yet _____, and _____ of expenses not yet _____.

Problem II.

For each of the following, enter the adjustment debits and credits in the adjustments column and extend the two account balances across to the adjusted trial balance column.

1. Adjustment (a): As of December 31, your company had used $100 of rent expense.

	Unadjusted Trial Balance		Adjustments		Adjusted Trial Balance		Income Statement		Balance Sheet	
	Dr	Cr	Dr	Cr	Dr	Cr	Dr	Cr	Dr	Cr
Cash										
Accounts Receivable										
Prepaid Rent	300									
Wages Payable										
Revenue										
Wages Expense										
Rent Expense										

2. Adjustment (b): The company had received and recorded a $10,000 advance on a $22,500 job, but as of December 31, had completed only 10% of the work.

| | Unadjusted Trial Balance | | Adjustments | | Adjusted Trial Balance | | Income Statement | | Balance Sheet | |
	Dr	Cr	Dr	Cr	Dr	Cr	Dr	Cr	Dr	Cr
Cash										
Accounts Receivable										
Prepaid Rent										
Wages Payable										
Unearned Revenue										
Revenue		10,000								
Wages Expense										
Rent Expense										

3. Adjustment (c): Wages Payable for the last week of the year were $10,000, and December 31 was on a Wednesday. Wages are paid each Friday.

| | Unadjusted Trial Balance | | Adjustments | | Adjusted Trial Balance | | Income Statement | | Balance Sheet | |
	Dr	Cr	Dr	Cr	Dr	Cr	Dr	Cr	Dr	Cr
Cash										
Accounts Receivable										
Prepaid Rent										
Wages Payable										
Unearned Revenue										
Revenue										
Wages Expense	495,000									
Rent Expense										

QUIZ 1   Solutions and Explanations

Problem I.

1. assets, liabilities, owners' equity, revenues, expenses

2. cut-off

3. earned, collected, incurred, paid

4. collection, earned, payment, incurred

Problem II.

1. Adjustment (a): At the cut-off date, your company had used $100 of rent expense.

	Unadjusted Trial Balance		Adjustments		Adjusted Trial Balance		Income Statement		Balance Sheet	
	Dr	**Cr**	**Dr**	**Cr**	**Dr**	**Cr**	**Dr**	**Cr**	**Dr**	**Cr**
Cash										
Accounts Receivable										
Prepaid Rent	300			(a) 100	200					
Wages Payable										
Revenue										
Wages Expense										
Rent Expense			(a) 100		100					

Explanation: You must reduce Prepaid Rent by the amount of rent expense incurred, which is $100. Thus, in the Adjustments column, Prepaid Rent is credited (reduced by) $100, and Rent Expense is debited (increased) by $100. The letter "(a)" is used to show that the credit to Prepaid Rent is part of the same adjustment as the debit to Rent Expense.

2. Adjustment (b): The company had received a $10,000 advance on a $22,500 job, but as of December 31 had completed only 10% of the work.

	Unadjusted Trial Balance		Adjustments		Adjusted Trial Balance		Income Statement		Balance Sheet	
	Dr	Cr	Dr	Cr	Dr	Cr	Dr	Cr	Dr	Cr
Cash										
Accounts Receivable										
Prepaid Rent										
Wages Payable										
Unearned Revenue				(b) 7,750		7,750				
Revenue		10,000	(b) 7,750			2,250				
Wages Expense										
Rent Expense										

Explanation: Because there is a balance in Revenue, but no balance in Unearned Revenue, it means that the entire advance payment was recorded to Revenue. Therefore, you must reduce the balance in Revenue by the amount not earned. To compute: $22,500 job x 10% completed = $2,250 earned. $10,000 advance – $2,250 earned = $7,750 reduction required in the balance of Revenue. Note that the percentage of the job completed is multiplied by the total cost of the job, not by the amount of the advance. The adjusted trial balance column shows that the ending balance in Unearned Revenue is $7,750, the amount that the company will earn in the future. The letter "(b)" in the adjustments column is used to show that the debit to Revenue is part of the same adjustment as the credit to Unearned Revenue.

3. Adjustment (c): Wages Payable for the last week of the year were $10,000, and December 31 was on a Wednesday.

	Unadjusted Trial Balance		Adjustments		Adjusted Trial Balance		Income Statement		Balance Sheet	
	Dr	**Cr**	**Dr**	**Cr**	**Dr**	**Cr**	**Dr**	**Cr**	**Dr**	**Cr**
Cash										
Accounts Receivable										
Prepaid Rent										
Wages Payable				(c) 6,000		6,000				
Unearned Revenue										
Revenue										
Wages Expense	495,000		(c) 6,000		501,000					
Rent Expense										

Explanation: If December 31 is on a Wednesday, the company incurred wages expense for 3 days of that week, Monday, Tuesday and Wednesday. This is 3/5 of the week. To compute: $10,000 weekly salary x 3/5 of the week = $6,000 wages expense incurred. In the Adjustments column, Wages Payable is credited for the $6,000 that the company owes for the week, and Wages Expense is debited for the $6,000 expense incurred for the week. The letter "(c)" is used to show that the debit to Wages Expense is part of the same adjustment as the credit to Wages Payable.

QUIZ 2   FROM UNADJUSTED TRIAL BALANCE TO FINANCIAL STATEMENTS

Problem I.

Multiple choice. Circle the correct answer.

1. Adjusting entries . . .

    a. record the receipt of cash
    b. always involve a liability account
    c. are necessary when the accrual basis of accounting is used
    d. always involve an asset account

2. Adjusting journal entries are usually recorded in the general journal . . .

    a. before they are entered on the worksheet
    b. after they are entered on the worksheet
    c. at the same time that they are entered on the worksheet
    d. either before or after they are entered on the worksheet as the preparer determines

3. Adjusting entries . . .

    a. never involve cash
    b. always involve cash
    c. may involve cash
    d. none of the above

Problem II.

For each of the following, enter the adjustment debits and credits in the adjustments column and extend the two account balances across to the adjusted trial balance column.

1. Adjustment (d): On December 31, management informs you that it has completed 10% of a $1,000 order on which it had received a $500 advance earlier in the year.

	Unadjusted Trial Balance		Adjustments		Adjusted Trial Balance		Income Statement		Balance Sheet	
	Dr	Cr	Dr	Cr	Dr	Cr	Dr	Cr	Dr	Cr
Cash										
Accounts Receivable										
Prepaid Rent										
Wages Payable										
Unearned Revenue		500								
Revenue										
Wages Expense										
Rent Expense										

2. Adjustment (e): Your company purchased office supplies earlier in the year. As of December 31, $100 in office supplies are still on hand.

	Unadjusted Trial Balance		Adjustments		Adjusted Trial Balance		Income Statement		Balance Sheet	
	Dr	**Cr**	**Dr**	**Cr**	**Dr**	**Cr**	**Dr**	**Cr**	**Dr**	**Cr**
Cash										
Accounts Receivable										
Prepaid Office Supplies										
Wages Payable										
Unearned Revenue										
Revenue										
Office Supplies Expense	400									
Rent Expense										

3. Adjustment (f): As of December 31, your company has used $1,000 of insurance.

	Unadjusted Trial Balance		Adjustments		Adjusted Trial Balance		Income Statement		Balance Sheet	
	Dr	**Cr**	**Dr**	**Cr**	**Dr**	**Cr**	**Dr**	**Cr**	**Dr**	**Cr**
Cash										
Accounts Receivable										
Prepaid Insurance	2,500									
Wages Payable										
Unearned Revenue										
Revenue										
Wages Expense										
Insurance Expense										

QUIZ 2 *Solutions and Explanations*

Problem I.

1. c

2. b

3. a

Problem II.

1. Adjustment (d): On December 31, management informs you that it has completed 10% of a $1,000 order on which it had received an advance earlier in the year.

	Unadjusted Trial Balance		Adjustments		Adjusted Trial Balance		Income Statement		Balance Sheet	
	Dr	Cr	Dr	Cr	Dr	Cr	Dr	Cr	Dr	Cr
Cash										
Accounts Receivable										
Prepaid Rent										
Wages Payable										
Unearned Revenue		500	(d) 100			400				
Revenue				(d) 100		100				
Wages Expense										
Rent Expense										

Explanation: You must reduce Unearned Revenue by the amount of revenue earned, which is $100 ($1,000 job x 10% completed). Thus, in the Adjustments column, Unearned Revenue is debited (reduced by) $100 and Revenue is credited (increased by) $100. The letter "(d)" is used to show that the debit to Unearned Revenue is part of the same adjustment as the credit to Revenue.

2. Adjustment (e): Your company purchased office supplies earlier in the year. As of December 31, $100 in office supplies are still on hand.

	Unadjusted Trial Balance		Adjustments			Adjusted Trial Balance		Income Statement		Balance Sheet	
	Dr	**Cr**	**Dr**	**Cr**		**Dr**	**Cr**	**Dr**	**Cr**	**Dr**	**Cr**
Cash											
Accounts Receivable											
Prepaid Office Supplies			(e) 100			100					
Wages Payable											
Unearned Revenue											
Revenue											
Office Supplies Expense	400			(e) 100		300					
Rent Expense											

Explanation: Because there is a balance in Office Supplies Expense, but no balance in Prepaid Office Supplies, the entire payment must have been recorded in Office Supplies Expense. Therefore, you must reduce the balance in Office Supplies Expense by the amount still on hand (not used up) at year end ($100). The adjusted trial balance shows that the ending balance in Prepaid Office Supplies is $100, the amount of supplies to be used in the future. The letter "(e)" is used to show that the debit to Prepaid Office Supplies is part of the same adjustment as the credit to Office Supplies Expense.

3. Adjustment (f): As of December 31, your company has used $1,000 in insurance expense.

	Unadjusted Trial Balance		Adjustments		Adjusted Trial Balance		Income Statement		Balance Sheet	
	Dr	**Cr**	**Dr**	**Cr**	**Dr**	**Cr**	**Dr**	**Cr**	**Dr**	**Cr**
Cash										
Accounts Receivable										
Prepaid Insurance	2,500			(f) 1,000	1,500					
Wages Payable										
Unearned Revenue										
Revenue										
Wages Expense										
Insurance Expense			(f) 1,000		1,000					

Explanation: Prepaid Insurance must be reduced by the $1,000 of insurance expense used up, and Insurance Expense must be increased by the same amount. Thus, Prepaid Insurance is credited for $1,000 and Insurance Expense is increased by the same amount. The adjustment leaves $1,500 in Prepaid Insurance to be used in the future.

Section 8

APPLYING YOUR KNOWLEDGE TO THE TRIAL BALANCE

In the two quizzes that follow, you will be given an unadjusted trial balance and the information for the year-end adjustments. To complete each worksheet:

1. Total the unadjusted trial balance debit and credit columns.

2. Compute and enter the adjustments on the worksheet and total the adjustments debit and credit columns.

3. Extend each line by combining the unadjusted trial balance and the adjustments and presenting the adjusted trial balance. Total the adjusted trial balance debits and credits to assure that they are in balance.

4. Record the journal entries in the general journal.

The following example explains each step.

EXAMPLE: You are given the following unadjusted trial balance:

		Unadjusted Trial Balance		Adjustments		Adjusted Trial Balance	
		Dr	Cr	Dr	Cr	Dr	Cr
100	Cash	10,000					
102	Accounts Receivable	25,000					
103	Allow./Doubtful Accts.		1,000				
201	InterestPayable						
220	Notes Payable		5,000				
300	Owner's Equity		10,000				
400	Sales		34,000				
511	Bad Debt Expense						
516	Interest Expense						
519	Salaries Expense	15,000					
	Total						

1. Total the debits and credits to make sure the sums are equal:

		Unadjusted Trial Balance		Adjustments		Adjusted Trial Balance	
		Dr	Cr	Dr	Cr	Dr	Cr
100	Cash	10,000					
102	Accounts Receivable	25,000					
103	Allow./Doubtful Accts.		1,000				
201	InterestPayable						
220	Notes Payable		5,000				
300	Owner's Equity		10,000				
400	Sales		34,000				
511	Bad Debt Expense						
516	Interest Expense						
519	Salaries Expense	15,000					
	Total	**50,000**	**50,000**				

2. Compute and enter the adjustments on the worksheet and total the adjustments debit and credit columns.

   (a) The firm has a $5,000 note, at 5% interest, payable annually.

   (b) The company estimates bad debt at 3% of credit sales; the portion of total sales that represents credit sales for the year is $10,000.

		Unadjusted Trial Balance		Adjustments		Adjusted Trial Balance	
		Dr	Cr	Dr	Cr	Dr	Cr
100	Cash	10,000					
102	Accounts Receivable	25,000					
103	Allow./Doubtful Accts.		1,000		(b) 300		
201	InterestPayable				(a) 250		
220	Notes Payable		5,000				
300	Owner's Equity		10,000				
400	Sales		34,000				
511	Bad Debt Expense			(b) 300			
516	Interest Expense			(a) 250			
519	Salaries Expense	15,000					
	Total	**50,000**	**50,000**	**550**	**550**		

3. Extend each line by combining the unadjusted trial balance and the adjustments on the adjusted trial balance. Total the adjusted trial balance debits and credits to assure that they are in balance.

		Unadjusted Trial Balance		Adjustments		Adjusted Trial Balance	
		Dr	Cr	Dr	Cr	Dr	Cr
100	Cash	25,000				25,000	
102	Accounts Receivable	10,000				10,000	
103	Allow./Doubtful Accts.		1,000		(b) 300		1,300
201	InterestPayable				(a) 250		250
220	Notes Payable		5,000				5,000
300	Owner's Equity		10,000				10,000
400	Sales		34,000				34,000
511	Bad Debt Expense			(b) 300		300	
516	Interest Expense			(a) 250		250	
519	Salaries Expense	15,000				15,000	
	Total	50,000	50,000	550	550	50,550	50,550

4. Record the journal entries in the general journal.

Interest Expense	250	
Interest Payable		250

To record accrued interest on note ($5,000 x 5%)

Bad Debt Expense	300	
Allowance For Doubtful Accounts		300

To record bad debt expense ($10,000 x 3%)

Do not use a computer spreadsheet; doing the quizzes manually provides a better review of the material.

QUIZ 1 APPLYING YOUR KNOWLEDGE
TO THE TRIAL BALANCE

Problem 1.

You are presented with the following unadjusted trial balance and year-end data:

Year-end data:

- Management estimates bad debt expense to be $16.

- The equipment has a 10-year life and no residual value, and is depreciated using the straight-line method.

- Insurance was taken out on January 1, 20X8 and prepaid for 18 months.

- The company received a $300 advance from BlaCo for a $750 job and completed 10% of the work by year end.

- Interest accrues on the notes payable at 10% per year, part of which has already been recorded.

Total the debits and credits in the unadjusted trial balance to make sure the sums are equal, then put a double underline beneath each sum. **(The answer is shown on page 122.)**

BC Company Worksheet
December 31, 20X8

		Unadjusted Trial Balance		Adjustments		Adjusted Trial Balance	
		Dr	Cr	Dr	Cr	Dr	Cr
100	Cash	500					
102	Receivables	850					
103	Allow./Doubtful Accts.		10				
105	Prepaid Insurance	600					
111	Equipment	1,000					
112	Accum. Depreciation		140				
200	Payables		200				
203	Unearned Revenue		300				
210	Notes Payable		800				
211	InterestPayable						
303A	Capital, A		500				
303B	Capital, B		500				
304A	Withdrawals, A	150					
304B	Withdrawals, B	150					
410	Revenue		2,100				
511	Bad Debt Expense						
512	Depreciation Expense						
514	Insurance Expense						
521	Rent Expense	150					
516	Interest Expense	20					
519	Salaries Expense	750					
520	Utility Expense	380					
	Total						

Solution to Problem I.

The debits and credits totals are equal.

		BC Company Worksheet December 31, 20X8					
		Unadjusted Trial Balance		Adjustments		Adjusted Trial Balance	
		Dr	Cr	Dr	Cr	Dr	Cr
100	Cash	500					
102	Receivables	850					
103	Allow./Doubtful Accts.		10				
105	Prepaid Insurance	600					
111	Equipment	1,000					
112	Accum. Depreciation		140				
200	Payables		200				
203	Unearned Revenue		300				
210	Notes Payable		800				
211	InterestPayable						
303A	Capital, A		500				
303B	Capital, B		500				
304A	Withdrawals, A	150					
304B	Withdrawals, B	150					
410	Revenue		2,100				
511	Bad Debt Expense						
512	Depreciation Expense						
514	Insurance Expense						
521	Rent Expense	150					
516	Interest Expense	20					
519	Salaries Expense	750					
520	Utility Expense	380					
	Total	**4,550**	**4,550**				

Check your answer: In addition to arriving at the same total debits and credits, did you remember to put a double-underline under both totals?

Problem II.

Year-end data (repeated for your convenience):

- Management estimates bad debt expense to be $16.

- The equipment has a 10-year life and no residual value, and is depreciated using the straight-line method.

- Insurance was taken out on January 1, 20X8 and prepaid for 18 months.

- The company received a $300 advance from BlaCo for a $750 job and completed 10% of the work by year end.

- Interest accrues on the notes payable at 10% per year, part of which has already been recorded.

Using the worksheet on page 125, compute the adjustments from the year-end data, and put the adjustments in the adjustments column.

Helpful hint: Remember that for each adjustment you must assign an alphabetical letter. For example, the first adjustment listed in the data is to Bad Debt Expense, so you would put an "(a)" next to the debit, and another "(a)" next to the credit. **(The answer is shown on page 126.)**

NOTES

BC Company Worksheet
December 31, 20X8

		Unadjusted Trial Balance		Adjustments		Adjusted Trial Balance	
		Dr	Cr	Dr	Cr	Dr	Cr
100	Cash	500					
102	Receivables	850					
103	Allow./Doubtful Accts.		10				
105	Prepaid Insurance	600					
111	Equipment	1,000					
112	Accum. Depreciation		140				
200	Payables		200				
203	Unearned Revenue		300				
210	Notes Payable		800				
211	InterestPayable						
303A	Capital, A		500				
303B	Capital, B		500				
304A	Withdrawals, A	150					
304B	Withdrawals, B	150					
410	Revenue		2,100				
511	Bad Debt Expense						
512	Depreciation Expense						
514	Insurance Expense						
521	Rent Expense	150					
516	Interest Expense	20					
519	Salaries Expense	750					
520	Utility Expense	380					
	Total	**4,550**	**4,550**				

Solution to Problem II.

The adjustments should appear as follows:

		BC Company Worksheet December 31, 20X8					
		Unadjusted Trial Balance		Adjustments		Adjusted Trial Balance	
		Dr	Cr	Dr	Cr	Dr	Cr
100	Cash	500					
102	Receivables	850					
103	Allow./Doubtful Accts.		10		(a) 16		
105	Prepaid Insurance	600			(c) 400		
111	Equipment	1,000					
112	Accum. Depreciation		140		(b) 100		
200	Payables		200				
203	Unearned Revenue		300	(d) 75			
210	Notes Payable		800				
211	InterestPayable				(e) 60		
303A	Capital, A		500				
303B	Capital, B		500				
304A	Withdrawals, A	150					
304B	Withdrawals, B	150					
410	Revenue		2,100		(d) 75		
511	Bad Debt Expense			(a) 16			
512	Depreciation Expense			(b) 100			
514	Insurance Expense			(c) 400			
521	Rent Expense	150					
516	Interest Expense	20		(e) 60			
519	Salaries Expense	750					
520	Utility Expense	380					
	Total	**4,550**	**4,550**	651	651		

The following computations are for instructional purposes. They do not appear with the worksheet.

(a) Management estimates bad debt to be $16.

(b) The equipment has a 10-year life and no residual value, and is depreciated using the straight-line method. To compute: $1,000 cost − $0 residual value = $1,000 depreciable base/10 years = $100 depreciation expense for the year.

(c) Insurance was prepaid on January 1, 20X8 for 18 months. To compute: $600 prepayment/18 months = $33.33 insurance expense/month x 12 months used in 20X8 = $400 insurance expense.

(d) The company received a $300 advance on a $750 job and com- pleted 10% of the work by year end. The fact that there is a $300 credit balance in Unearned Revenue means that the entire $300 advance was credited to Unearned Revenue. As of year-end, BC had completed 10% of the job, so Revenue must include $75; the remainder must remain in Unearned Revenue. To compute: $750 job x 10% completed (earned) = $75 earned.

(e) Interest accrues on the notes payable at 10% per year, of which $20 has already been paid. To compute: $800 notes payable x 10% interest = $80 interest for the year − $20 interest paid = $60 additional interest expense.

To check your answers: Did you arrive at the same total debits and credits in the adjustments column? Did you put a double underline under each total? Did you link each debit with its correct credit (i.e., use the same letter for both), even if you used different letters from the ones printed above?

Problem III.

On the worksheet on page 129, extend each line by combining the unadjusted trial balance and the adjustments on the adjusted trial balance. Total the adjusted trial balance debits and credits to assure that they are in balance. **(The answer is shown on page 130.)**

Problem IV.

Now, show how the adjustments are recorded in the general journal. **(The answer is shown on page 131.)**

BC Company Worksheet
December 31, 20X8

		Unadjusted Trial Balance		Adjustments		Adjusted Trial Balance	
		Dr	Cr	Dr	Cr	Dr	Cr
100	Cash	500					
102	Receivables	850					
103	Allow./Doubtful Accts.		10		(a) 16		
105	Prepaid Insurance	600			(c) 400		
111	Equipment	1,000					
112	Accum. Depreciation		140		(b) 100		
200	Payables		200				
203	Unearned Revenue		300	(d) 75			
210	Notes Payable		800				
211	InterestPayable				(e) 60		
303A	Capital, A		500				
303B	Capital, B		500				
304A	Withdrawals, A	150					
304B	Withdrawals, B	150					
410	Revenue		2,100		(d) 75		
511	Bad Debt Expense			(a) 16			
512	Depreciation Expense			(b) 100			
514	Insurance Expense			(c) 400			
521	Rent Expense	150					
516	Interest Expense	20		(e) 60			
519	Salaries Expense	750					
520	Utility Expense	380					
	Total	**4,550**	**4,550**	651	651		

Solution to Problem III.

Here is what BC Company's worksheet should look like:

BC Company Worksheet
December 31, 20X8

		Unadjusted Trial Balance		Adjustments		Adjusted Trial Balance	
		Dr	Cr	Dr	Cr	Dr	Cr
100	Cash	500				500	
102	Receivables	850				850	
103	Allow./Doubtful Accts.		10		(a) 16		26
105	Prepaid Insurance	600			(c) 400	200	
111	Equipment	1,000				1,000	
112	Accum. Depreciation				(b) 100		240
200	Payables		140				200
203	Unearned Revenue		200	(d) 75			225
210	Notes Payable		300				800
211	Interest Payable		800		(e) 60		60
303A	Capital, A						500
303B	Capital, B		500				500
304A	Withdrawals, A	150	500			150	
304B	Withdrawals, B	150				150	
410	Revenue				(d) 75		2,175
511	Bad Debt Expense		2,100	(a) 16		16	
512	Depreciation Expense			(b) 100		100	
514	Insurance Expense			(c) 400		400	
521	Rent Expense	150				150	
516	Interest Expense	20		(e) 60		80	
519	Salaries Expense	750				750	
520	Utility Expense	380				380	
	Total	4,550	4,550	651	651	4,726	4,726

The adjustments are recorded in the general journal as follows:

    (a) Bad Debt Expense   16

           Allowance For Doubtful Accounts   16

           To record bad debt expense

    (b) Depreciation Expense   100

           Accumulated Depreciation   100

           To accrue depreciation expense

    (c) Insurance Expense   400

           Prepaid Insurance   400

           To accrue insurance expense

    (d) Unearned Revenue   75

           Revenue   75

           To recognize revenue for Blaco job

    (e) Interest Expense   60

           Interest Payable   60

           To accrue interest expense on notes payable

Check your answers: Did you put a letter next to each journal entry that corresponds to the same adjustment on the trial balance (in the adjustments column)? Did you put a brief descriptive explanation under each entry (in italics on the printed answer)? Did you copy correctly the amount of each debit or credit? Did you total the debits and credits in three places (adjusted trial balance, adjustments and unadjusted trial balance)? When you extended each line to the adjusted trial balance, did your addition and subtraction give the answer printed in the adjusted trial balance column? Did your totals in the adjusted trial balance debit and credit columns match the printed ones? Did you put a double-underline under each total?

QUIZ 2 APPLYING YOUR KNOWLEDGE TO THE TRIAL BALANCE

Problem I.

You are presented with the following unadjusted trial balance and year-end data:

Think Inc. Worksheet
December 31, 20X8

		Unadjusted Trial Balance		Adjustments		Adjusted Trial Balance	
		Dr	**Cr**	**Dr**	**Cr**	**Dr**	**Cr**
100	Cash	400					
104	Accounts Receivable	900					
105	Allow./Doubtful Accts.		20				
106	Prepaid Rent						
108	Inventory	800					
113	Equipment	1,300					
118	Accum. Depreciation		200				
205	Accounts Payable		380				
208	Salaries Payable						
300	Common Stock		1,200				
305	Retained Earnings		1,500				
400	Sales		2,500				
500	Cost of Sales	1,000					
512	Depreciation Expense						
514	Insurance Expense	250					
516	Bad Dept Expense						
518	Salaries Expense	750					
521	Rent Expense	400					
	Total						

Year-end data:

- Management estimates that 3% of accounts receivable will not be collected.
- The company depreciates the equipment under the straight-line method. The equipment has a $300 residual value and a 5-year life.
- On December 1, the company prepaid rent of $400 for 4 months.
- Salaries of $50 have accrued, but have not been paid.

Complete the worksheet as follows:

1. Total the unadjusted trial balance debit and credit columns.

2. Compute and enter the adjustments on the worksheet and total the adjustments debit and credit columns.

3. Extend each line by combining the unadjusted trial balance and the adjustments on the adjusted trial balance. Total the adjusted trial balance debits and credits to assure that they are in balance.

4. Write the journal entries that will be recorded in the general journal.

Do not turn to the answer page until you have completed all four of the above steps. (All of the answers are shown on pages 134 and 135.)

Solution to Problem I.

Here is what Think, Inc.'s worksheet should look like:

Think Inc. Worksheet
December 31, 20X8

		Unadjusted Trial Balance		Adjustments		Adjusted Trial Balance	
		Dr	**Cr**	**Dr**	**Cr**	**Dr**	**Cr**
100	Cash	400				400	
104	Accounts Receivable	900				900	
105	Allow./Doubtful Accts.		20		(a) 7		27*
106	Prepaid Rent			(c) 300		300	
108	Inventory	800				800	
113	Equipment	1,300				1,300	
118	Accum. Depreciation		200		(b) 200		400
205	Accounts Payable		380				380
208	Salaries Payable				(d) 50		50
300	Common Stock		1,200				1,200
305	Retained Earnings		1,500				1,500
400	Sales		2,500				2,500
500	Cost of Sales	1,000				1,000	
512	Depreciation Expense			(b) 200		200	
514	Insurance Expense	250				250	
516	Bad Dept Expense			(a) 7		7	
518	Salaries Expense	750		(d) 50		800	
521	Rent Expense	400			(c) 300	100	
	Total	**5,800**	**5,800**	**557**	**557**	**6,057**	**6,057**

*Under the percentage of accounts receivable method for recording bad debt, the year-end balance in the Allowance For Doubtful Accounts must be $27. Becaue the balance in the Allowance For Doubtful Accounts was $20, it had to be increased by (credited for) $7 to arrive at the correct ending balance of $27.

The adjustments are recorded in the general journal as follows:

(a) Bad Debt Expense   7
     Allowance For Doubtful Accounts   7
    To record bad debt expense

(b) Depreciation Expense   200
     Accumulated Depreciation   200
    To accrue depreciation expense

(c) Prepaid Rent   300
     Rent Expense   300
    To adjust the balance in Rent Expense

(d) Salaries Expense   50
     Salaries Payable   50
    To accrue salaries expense

Check your answers: Did you total the debits and credits in three places (adjusted trial balance, adjustments and unadjusted trial balance)? Did you put a double-underline under each total? Did you link each debit with its correct credit (i.e., use the same letter for both) and again with the general journal entry? (You may use any letters as long as you link the debit, credit and journal entry properly.) When you extended each line to the adjusted trial balance, did your addition and subtraction give the answer printed in the adjusted trial balance column?

NOTES

MASTERING ADJUSTING ENTRIES

Instructions: Detach the Final Examination Answer Sheet on page 147 before beginning your final examination. Select the correct letter for each answer below, then fill it in on the Answer Sheet. Allow approximately 2 hours.

1. A chart of accounts lists accounts in the following order . . .

    a. income, expense, asset, liability and owners' equity accounts.
    b. asset, income, expense, liability and owners' equity accounts.
    c. asset, income, owners' equity, expense and liability accounts.
    d. asset, liability, owners' equity, income and expense accounts.

2. On which of the following accounts do we normally *not* record depreciation?

    a. Inventory
    b. Equipment
    c. Furniture
    d. Building

3. Interest earned on a money market account and credited to your company's bank account but not recorded on your books . . .

    a. is recorded on your books with a normal transaction entry.
    b. is recorded on your books with an adjusting entry.
    c. is recorded on your books with both a transaction entry and an adjusting entry.
    d. requires no entry in your books.

4. Which of the following dates is appropriate for a profit and loss statement?

    a. as of June 30, 20XX
    b. June 30, 20XX
    c. for the Quarter Ended June 30, 20XX
    d. All of the above are appropriate.

5. Total debits must equal total credits. This is the basis of . . .

    a. an income statement.
    b. an earnings statement.
    c. a profit and loss statement.
    d. double-entry bookkeeping.

6. Which of the following accounts might be included in an adjusting entry?

    a. Cash
    b. Buildings
    c. Insurance Expense
    d. all of the above

7. Which of the following is an asset?

    a. Payables
    b. Unearned Revenue
    c. Receivables
    d. Revenue

8. On the accrual basis, revenue is recorded when it is . . .

    a. received.   b. earned.   c. incurred.   d. paid.

9. On the cash basis, expenses are recorded when they are . . .

    a. received.   b. earned.   c. incurred.   d. paid.

10. Your company gets $5,000 in December to paint a house. The work is done in January. How much revenue is reported on a cash basis in December and January, respectively?

    a. $2,500 and $2,500
    b. $5,000 and $0
    c. $0 and $5,000
    d. $2,000 and $3,000

11. You receive $80,000 before you do work for a customer. The journal entry to record this transaction is . . .

a. Cash   80,000
     Unearned Revenue   80,000
To record cash received

b. Cash   80,000
     Accounts Receivable   80,000
To record cash received

c. Cash   80,000
     Accounts Payable   80,000
To record cash received

d. Unearned Revenue   80,000
     Cash   80,000
To record cash received

12. When are adjusting entries prepared?

a. beginning of the accounting period
b. end of the accounting period
c. middle of the accounting period
d. time of the transaction

13. Your company holds a 90-day note receivable of $10,000 from a customer. The note is dated October 31 and has a 12% interest rate. Your company's year ends on December 31. How much interest revenue do you accrue on December 31?

a. $1,200   b. $300   c. $200   d. $0

14. The journal entry to accrue interest revenue is . . .

a. Cash
    Interest Revenue
    To accrue interest

c. Interest Receivable
    Interest Revenue
    To accrue interest

b. Interest Revenue
    Cash
    To accrue interest

d. Interest Revenue
    Interest Receivable
    To accrue interest

15. Your company sells a product for another company and receives a commission of 10% on sales. By the end of your company's fiscal year, your company had sales of $200,000 and received $8,000, which was credited to Revenue. How much additional revenue must be recorded this fiscal year?

a. $20,000   b. $12,000   c. $8,000   d. $0

16. When revenue is accrued, what is the effect on assets and income, respectively?

a. Both increase.
b. Both decrease.
c. Assets increase; income decreases.
d. Assets decrease; income increases.

17. Which of the following is an accurate description of accrued revenue?

a. It is unearned.
b. It has been received in cash.
c. It is earned and received in cash.
d. It has not yet been received in cash.

18. The balance in Allowance For Doubtful Accounts is important to the calculation of bad debt when bad debt is calculated . . .

a. as a percentage of credit sales.
b. as a percentage of accounts receivable that will not be collected.
c. under the direct write-off method.
d. none of the above.

19. A company with a 5-day workweek pays employees on Friday. Its accounting period ends on Thursday. Gross salary for the week is $10,000. How much salary expense is accrued at year end?

    a. $10,000   b. $8,000   c. $2,000   d. $0

20. Which of the following journal entries accrues interest expense?

    a. Interest Expense   c. Interest Expense
          Interest Payable   Cash
        To accrue interest expense   *To accrue interest expense*

    b. Interest Payable   d. Cash
          Interest Expense   Interest Expense
        To accrue interest expense   *To accrue interest expense*

21. A firm with a 6-day workweek pays employees on Saturday. If the firm's year ends on a Saturday, and gross salary for that week is $12,000, how much salary expense is accrued at year end?

    a. $12,000   b. $8,000   c. $6,000   d. $0

22. Your company's year ends on May 31. On May 1, it borrowed $50,000 for 1 year at 12% interest. How much interest expense has it accrued on May 31?

    a. $6,000   b. $5,000   c. $500   d. $0

23. With accrued expenses, cash payment follows recording the expense.

    a. True   b. False

24. What type of account is Deferred Commissions?

    a. expense   b. asset   c. liability   d. revenue

25. Your company pays expenses of $50,000 during the year and accrues expenses of $5,000 at year end. What are your company's total expenses for the year?

    a. $55,000   b. $50,000   c. $45,000   d. $5,000

The following information relates to questions 26, 27, and 28: Rehabilitation, Inc. uses accrual basis accounting. It collects $10,000 in December for a painting job and credits revenue. By the end of December, its year end, the company has completed 30% of the job.

26. How much cash did Rehabilitation, Inc. collect in December?

    a. $10,000   b. $7,000   c. $3,000   d. $0

27. How much revenue has Rehabilitation, Inc. earned in December?

    a. $10,000   b. $7,000   c. $3,000   d. $0

28. The adjusting journal entry on December 31 (omitting dollars) is . . .

    a. Unearned Revenue   c. Revenue
          Cash   Unearned Revenue
        To reflect unearned revenue   *To reflect unearned revenue*

    b. Unearned Revenue   d. Cash
          Revenue   Revenue
        To reflect unearned revenue   *To reflect unearned revenue*

29. Unearned revenue is also known as . . .

    a. deferred expense.
    b. deferred revenue.
    c. earned revenue.
    d. cash paid.

30. The Cash ledger account is not used in adjusting entries.

    a. True   b. False

The following information relates to questions 31 and 32: CBA Co. uses accrual basis accounting. It collects $20,000 in December for a job and credits unearned revenue. By the end of December, its year end, CBA has completed 40% of the work.

31. How much revenue has CBA earned in December?

    a. $20,000   b. $12,000   c. $8,000   d. $0

32. Which accounts does CBA debit and credit in the adjusting journal entry on December 31?

    a. Unearned Revenue   c. Revenue
          Cash   Unearned Revenue
      To reflect revenue earned   *To reflect revenue earned*

    b. Unearned Revenue   d. Cash
          Revenue   Revenue
      To reflect revenue earned   *To reflect revenue earned*

33. When revenue is credited, it increases revenue.

    a. True   b. False

34. Unearned Revenue is what type of account?

    a. asset   b. liability   c. revenue   d. expense

35. In accrual basis accounting, "recognized" would mean . . .

    a. paid.   b. received.   c. incurred.   d. recorded.

36. With prepaid supplies, cash payment follows recording of the expense.

    a. True   b. False

The following information relates to questions 37, 38, and 39: DEF Co. uses accrual basis accounting. It pays $15,000 to cover a 3-year insurance premium and debits "insurance expense." One (1) year has elapsed.

37. How much insurance expense has DEF Co. incurred this year?

a. $15,000   b. $10,000   c. $5,000   d. $0

38. How much has DEF Co. paid for insurance this year?

a. $15,000   b. $10,000   c. $5,000   d. $0

39. What is the adjusting journal entry (omitting dollars) after 1 year?

a. Insurance Expense
        Cash
    To record prepaid insurance

c. Prepaid Insurance
        Insurance Expense
    To record prepaid insurance

b. Insurance Expense
        Prepaid Insurance
    To record prepaid insurance

d. Prepaid Insurance
        Cash
    To record prepaid insurance

40. What type of account is Prepaid Insurance?

a. asset   b. liability   c. revenue   d. expense

41. Your company buys office supplies and debits Supplies On Hand for $10,000. At year end, you estimate that you used $4,000 of these supplies. What is the expense for supplies used?

a. $10,000   b. $6,000   c. $4,000   d. $0

42. Generally, an adjusting journal entry . . .

a. is used in both accrual basis and cash basis accounting.
b. affects both the income statement and the balance sheet.
c. affects only the income statement.
d. affects only the balance sheet.

43. Your company, which uses accrual basis accounting, pays $18,000 in advance to cover a 3-year insurance premium and debits Prepaid Insurance. How much insurance expense has your company incurred after 1 year has elapsed?

      a. $18,000   b. $12,000   c. $6,000   d. $0

Use the following information for Questions 44 and 45: Your company shows the following data at the end of its first year:

Credit sales for the year	$1,000,000
Accounts Receivable balance	100,000
Allowance for Doubtful Accounts	4,000 credit balance

44. If bad debt is estimated as 1% of credit sales, the adjusting entry for bad debt expense includes a debit for . . .

      a. $14,000.   b. $10,000.   c. $6,000.   d. $0.

45. If your company estimates that it will not collect 5% of its accounts receivable, the year-end adjustment to Allowance For Doubtful Accounts will be . . .

      a. a credit of $1,000.
      b. a credit of $5,000.
      c. a debit of $1,000.
      d. a debit of $5,000.

46. If December 1, your company opens for business and leases space in a building for $1,000 per month and pays 3 months' rent in advance. On December 31, the balance in Rent Expense is $3,000, it means that the advance payment for rent was recorded in . . .

      a. Prepaid Rent, which must now be credited for $1,000.
      b. Rent Expense, which must now be credited for $2,000.
      c. Prepaid Rent, which must now be debited for $1,000.
      d. Rent Expense, which must now be debited for $2,000.

47. Your company accrued $20,000 of salary expense at the end of Year 1, then paid $30,000 of salaries early in Year 2. How much salary expense applies to Years 1 and 2, respectively?

    a. $30,000 and $0
    b. $0 and $30,000
    c. $10,000 and $20,000
    d. $20,000 and $10,000

Use the following information to answer Questions 48–50:

	Unadjusted Trial Balance		Adjustments		Adjusted Trial Balance	
	Dr	**Cr**	**Dr**	**Cr**	**Dr**	**Cr**
Accounts Receivable	40,000					
Allowance for Doubtful Accounts	2,000					
Supplies on Hand	800					
Utilities Payable		6,000				
Notes Payable		10,000				
Bad Debt Expense						
Supplies Expense	2,300			800		
Utilities Expense	8,000		1,000			

48. If the partial adjustment shown for Utilities Expense is correct, what would be the adjusted trial balance amount for Utilities Payable?

    a. $1,000 debit
    b. $4,000 credit
    c. $6,000 debit
    d. $7,000 credit

49. If the adjustment shown for Supplies Expense is correct, what is the adjusted trial balance amount for Supplies on Hand?

    a. $800   b. $1,600   c. $2,400   d. $0

50. If the company estimates that it will not be able to collect 3% of accounts receivable, the debit to Bad Debt Expense in the adjustments column is . . .

    a. $3,200.   b. $2,000.   c. $1,200.   d. $0.

Final Examination Answer Sheet
MASTERING ADJUSTING ENTRIES

Instructions: Detach this sheet before starting the Final Exam. For each question, check the box beneath the letter of the correct answer. Use a pen or a #2 pencil to make a dark impression. When completed, return to: AIPB Continuing Education, Suite 500, 6001 Montrose Road, Rockville, MD 20852. If you attain a grade of at least 70, you will receive the Institute's *Certificate of Completion*. Answer Sheets are not returned.

Certified Bookkeeper applicants: If you attain a grade of at least 70, and become certified within 3 years of passing this exam, you will receive retroactively six (6) Continuing Professional Education Credits (CPECs) toward your *Certified Bookkeeper* CPEC requirements.

	a	b	c	d		a	b	c	d		a	b	c	d		a	b	c	d
1.	☐	☐	☐	☐	14.	☐	☐	☐	☐	27.	☐	☐	☐	☐	39.	☐	☐	☐	☐
2.	☐	☐	☐	☐	15.	☐	☐	☐	☐	28.	☐	☐	☐	☐	40.	☐	☐	☐	☐
3.	☐	☐	☐	☐	16.	☐	☐	☐	☐	29.	☐	☐	☐	☐	41.	☐	☐	☐	☐
4.	☐	☐	☐	☐	17.	☐	☐	☐	☐	30.	☐	☐	☐	☐	42.	☐	☐	☐	☐
5.	☐	☐	☐	☐	18.	☐	☐	☐	☐	31.	☐	☐	☐	☐	43.	☐	☐	☐	☐
6.	☐	☐	☐	☐	19.	☐	☐	☐	☐	32.	☐	☐	☐	☐	44.	☐	☐	☐	☐
7.	☐	☐	☐	☐	20.	☐	☐	☐	☐	33.	☐	☐	☐	☐	45.	☐	☐	☐	☐
8.	☐	☐	☐	☐	21.	☐	☐	☐	☐	34.	☐	☐	☐	☐	46.	☐	☐	☐	☐
9.	☐	☐	☐	☐	22.	☐	☐	☐	☐	35.	☐	☐	☐	☐	47.	☐	☐	☐	☐
10.	☐	☐	☐	☐	23.	☐	☐	☐	☐	36.	☐	☐	☐	☐	48.	☐	☐	☐	☐
11.	☐	☐	☐	☐	24.	☐	☐	☐	☐	37.	☐	☐	☐	☐	49.	☐	☐	☐	☐
12.	☐	☐	☐	☐	25.	☐	☐	☐	☐	38.	☐	☐	☐	☐	50.	☐	☐	☐	☐
13.	☐	☐	☐	☐	26.	☐	☐	☐	☐										

Name _____   Title _____

Company _____   Street Address _____

City _____   State _____   Zip _____   Phone Number _____

Email Address (Important) (Please print clearly.) _____

For *Certified Bookkeeper* applicants only: #_____
Membership or Certification (nonmember) ID Number

NOTES

Course Evaluation for
MASTERING ADJUSTING ENTRIES

Please complete and return (even if you do not take the Final Examination) to: AIPB Continuing Education, Suite 500, 6001 Montrose Road, Rockville, MD 20852. **PLEASE PRINT CLEARLY.**

Circle one

1. Did you find the instructions clear?   Yes   No

Comments: _____

2. Did you find the course practical?   Yes   No

Comments_____

3. Is this course what you expected?   Yes   No

Comments_____

4. Would you recommend this course to other accounting professionals?   Yes   No

Comments: _____

5. What did you like most about *Mastering Adjusting Entries*?

_____

6. What would have made the course even more helpful?

_____

7. May we use your comments and name in advertising for the course?   Yes   No

8. Would you be interested in other courses?   Yes   No

Please indicate what subject areas would be of greatest interest to you:

1. _____   3. _____

2. _____   4. _____

Name (optional)	Title		
Company	Street Address		
City	State	Zip	Phone Number